CHINESE IN NAPA VALLEY

CHINESE IN NAPA VALLEY

THE FORGOTTEN COMMUNITY THAT BUILT WINE COUNTRY

JOHN McCORMICK

FOREWORD BY CONNIE YOUNG YU

THE
History
PRESS

Published by The History Press
Charleston, SC
www.historypress.com

First published 2023

Manufactured in the United States

ISBN 9781467152785

Library of Congress Control Number: 2022944977

Notice: The information in this book is true and complete to the best of our knowledge. It is offered without guarantee on the part of the author or The History Press. The author and The History Press disclaim all liability in connection with the use of this book.

This book is dedicated to the countless Chinese people who lived and worked in the Napa Valley between 1870 and 1900. You worked so hard, and we should have treated you much better.

CONTENTS

FOREWORD

The character of Napa Valley wine is defined in terms of European viticulture, and Chinese in straw hats working in all stages of winemaking does not fit this celebrated image. Yet it is a fact that the wine industry in Napa was established by a labor force of men from Guangdong Province, China.

In this book, John McCormick tells how Chinese were essential to winemaking in Napa and other industries as well. They worked on the railroads, in quicksilver mines, in tanneries and on hop farms. They built bridges, stone fences and roadways. They were domestic servants, laundrymen, gardeners and cooks. They were indispensable to the life of Napa.

Northern California winemakers depended on them for many tasks, just as Chinese were needed to build the western portion of the transcontinental railroad from 1864 to 1869. As a descendant of railroad worker Lee Wong Sang, I am proud that his kinfolk found work in the vineyards after the driving of the last spike at Promontory, Utah. Chinese did the same dangerous work in building the caves at Schramsberg Winery in Calistoga as they did building tunnels in the Sierra Nevada Mountains, using hand tools and explosives.

Chinese workers had a life, as this book describes. They enjoyed being in the splendid new land, while having the food of their native country, its rich culture and traditions. They had camaraderie at work camp, with the common purpose of earning enough wages to send money to their families in China. Every Chinatown was a home base where the worker would get news and mail, visit with the merchants and their families, worship at the Taoist altar and gamble. They knew of their importance to the vineyard owners, and they held economic power. Several times they struck for better wages and won their demands. But then they would face the siege of their lives: the anti-Chinese movement of the 1880s, led by powerful white labor and political forces sweeping the West. It was a reign of sanctioned terror unparalleled in American history.

John McCormick documents how every city in Napa Valley was involved in the organized movement to expel Chinese in the 1880s. Anti-Chinese events were led by city councilmen and sheriffs. The statewide Anti-Chinese League had branches in all municipalities of Napa. In a suspenseful narrative, McCormick describes how each city took a different approach in handling the "Chinese Problem," from an economic boycott to legal harassment to a march on Chinatown. Avoiding the use of force, as did many cities in the West, the Napa authorities could not make the Chinese leave. Vineyard owners protested that without Chinese workers, they would lose their grape harvest. The entire agricultural industry of Napa was dependent on Chinese, and it would be economic disaster for the Valley if they were expelled. Thus, while the anti-Chinese movement was unsuccessful in expelling Chinese, it did succeed in making life miserable for them here. They would never be allowed to be citizens, own land and settle down in Napa. From vegetable peddler to laundryman, the Chinese were harassed and bullied going about their daily lives.

The passage of the Chinese Exclusion Law in 1882 was a defining moment in America's history. The law excluded Chinese laborers for ten years and ruled that a race of people, the Chinese, be prohibited from naturalization to citizenship. The Geary Act of 1892 extended the exclusion of Chinese laborers for another ten years and required every Chinese man, woman and child to register and be photographed for a Certificate of Residence. I have the chak chee of my grandfather Yung Wah Gok, with the stamp of "laborer." He had to carry it at all times or else face arrest and deportation. He came to San Jose's Market Street Chinatown as an eleven-year-old worker in 1881, one year before the Chinese Exclusion Act. Going outside his home base, rocks would be thrown at him by white boys. On May 4, 1887, while working in the strawberry fields, Yung saw his Chinatown destroyed by a massive fire. He would tell his son, my father, who told me, "It was set by white people to drive us out."

This book by John McCormick shows how the ugly, cruel anti-Chinese movement could happen in beautiful, tranquil Napa Valley. Citizens incited by racist propaganda felt that it was their patriotic duty to rid their communities of "Yellow Peril," and the Napa newspapers of the time filled with anti-Chinese bias. John McCormick digs deep into archival records and uses the few oral histories available for the point of view of the Chinese. While Chinese challenged unjust laws and resisted expulsion, there was no way they could eventually prevail. The local anti-Chinese movement, propelled by national exclusion laws, decimated the Chinese working population, ultimately driving the Chinese from the vineyards in the Valley and ending their Chinatowns.

With the exception of the caves at Schramsberg in Calistoga and at Buena Vista in Sonoma, we have little physical evidence remaining of the Chinese contributions to the wine country. But there is documentation. No one who reads this book will ever again sip a glass of Napa wine without being reminded of the Chinese who planted the vineyards and harvested and processed the grapes but were denied a place at the table.

CONNIE YOUNG YU,
Author, *Chinatown, San Jose, USA*

PREFACE

I grew up in Napa and spent the first eighteen years of my life thinking that it was perfectly normal to have thousands of tourists descend on my hometown every weekend. As children in Napa schools, we learned about local history. We learned about the Native Americans who populated the Napa Valley for thousands of years before the arrival of European immigrants. These included people historians call the Wappo and Southern Patwin tribes, although they called themselves names like Mishewal, Mutistil and Meyakama. As schoolchildren, we would take field trips to Glass Mountain, a volcanic peak south of Howell Mountain near St. Helena, to see the obsidian covering the mountainside and try to find arrowheads left by the Wappo. We learned about the California Missions founded by Franciscan priests and the arrival of the Spanish to claim land around Napa in the late eighteenth and early nineteenth centuries. We also learned about George Yount, for whom Yountville is named, who got one of the first land grants for a white European in the Napa Valley in 1836.

From that point on, local history was mostly about white Europeans settling and developing the area. At no time that I recall were Chinese ever mentioned. I had no idea that they were an integral part of Napa Valley history or how they were treated. Their contributions were ignored or lost in the overall narrative of Manifest Destiny. Yet their story and accomplishments are as interesting, varied and remarkable as any group of people we learned about in school. They are more important than many groups because, as we will see, most of the economic activities that formed the foundation for the modern

Napa Valley could not have been done without the Chinese workforce. Yet even now there are very few monuments, markers or acknowledgement of the Chinese contribution to the Napa Valley. Hopefully this book will help introduce the role of the Chinese worker to the public and, eventually, to a new generation of schoolchildren.

ACKNOWLEDGEMENTS

The inspiration for this book grew from an article Research Director Mariam Hansen wrote on the St. Helena Historical Society's website in which she discussed the contributions of Chinese workers in St. Helena in the late 1800s. Her knowledge in this area was very inspiring. I am grateful to the Chinese Historical Society of America (CHSA) for allowing me to present this work while in progress and providing excellent feedback and encouragement to continue my research and eventually publish a book. I especially want to acknowledge Joyce Chan of CHSA for her enthusiasm for the topic of Chinese in the Napa Valley and helping me make connections in the Chinese American historical community.

Erez Manela, professor of history at Harvard, provided an excellent foundation of the history of U.S./China immigration that served as the starting point for this project, and he was an incredibly supportive thesis director. Jenny Banh, associate professor of anthropology and Asian studies at California State University–Fresno, pushed me to transform the thesis topic into a book and provided invaluable guidance in the pros and cons of academic versus general history publishing.

I have met some fascinating and inspirational people during the journey to publish this book. Jack Jue worked very hard, along with his Auntie Soo-Yin Jue, on a family blog that documented the oral history of his great-grandfather Jue Joe. Jack did a lot of research himself to reconcile and corroborate facts about Jue Joe's life. He graciously allowed me to use Jue Joe's story and family pictures in this book. I thank Kelly O'Connor, the research librarian for the Napa County Historical Society, for her work in helping me gather and sift through the archive material at the society, even during the height of pandemic restrictions. I also appreciate the work of Kara Brunzell, an architectural historian and a fellow researcher of Chinese in the Napa Valley, who graciously shared many of the images and resources she used in her investigations. I was also fortunate to connect with Robin Leong, the president of the Vallejo Napa Chinese Club, who had been trying for years to get a much-improved plaque on Napa's First Street Bridge that better described the Chinese contributions to Napa. His passion for and tenacity in that project helped me understand and appreciate the noble purpose of this book.

I am thankful to Hugh Davies, owner of Schramsberg Winery, and marketing manager Matthew Levy for providing a remarkable on-site tour of the wine caves dug by Chinese workers and the "Chinese Bunkhouse" still on site and largely unchanged from when it was used to house them. It is one of the few large-scale physical artifacts still present today that help us better understand the daily life of the Chinese laborer.

I am profoundly indebted to Connie Young Yu, who not only agreed to write the foreword but also provided amazing feedback on many key areas of the book, including the literacy of many of the Chinese immigrants, a topic that is frequently glossed over by historians. She also helped frame the contributions of the Chinese Six Companies to the lives of Chinese immigrants and clarified the relationships between Chinese labor bosses and their workers, the role of community in the lives of the Chinese workers and the role of Chinese women immigrants. Her respect for and admiration of the Chinese workers who are discussed in this book is inspiring.

I am forever grateful to my wife, Colleen, who graciously put up with untold hours of me sequestered in the office writing or in the Napa Valley doing research. Her unwavering support of me and this project is unbelievable. Finally, I am deeply thankful to Scott McCormick, who helped edit many of the papers that led up to this publication, and Emily McCormick, who provided innumerable detailed and thoughtful edits and suggestions for this book. The fact that the two best editors one could wish for also happen to be my children is purely coincidental. Any errors that remain are mine alone.

INTRODUCTION

California's Napa Valley is one of the most famous wine-growing regions in the world. Its 475 wineries typically draw almost 4 million visitors per year and contribute more than $34 billion annually to the U.S. economy.[1] The wine industry in this region from 1870 through 1900 was built predominantly using Chinese immigrant labor. These laborers were unable to become citizens and were largely confined to local Chinatowns that were mostly collections of poorly built structures in less desirable parts of town. The Chinese powered a significant portion of the Napa Valley economy and worked not only in vineyards and wineries but also in quicksilver mines, on farms, for local railroads, as shopkeepers, as hired laborers and as domestic help. Despite their essential role in Napa Valley society, the Chinese were hated, feared and threatened by many locals, especially white men who felt that well-paying jobs were being taken away from them. Once most of the Chinese laborers were finally driven out of the region around 1900, their homes and businesses were razed, and most of their contributions, even their very presence, were largely forgotten.

This book seeks to examine and document how this Chinese immigrant community in the Napa Valley survived and even prospered for more than thirty years in the late nineteenth century despite the intense level of discrimination at the national, state and local levels. How did they interact with citizens and local law enforcement that viewed them as illegitimate and unwanted yet necessary to the community's well-being? What broader immigration and demographic forces eventually compelled them to leave, and why were their contributions forgotten? How did they form a community for financial, social and spiritual support? The Napa Valley Chinese were truly "impossible subjects" whom many felt should not be allowed to live in the same town as white citizens and/or integrate into society, yet they were critical to the economic success of the entire region.[2] We will discover that the Chinese workers contributed extensively to the economy through a variety of jobs in some of the largest industries in the Napa Valley and used the Chinatowns of the various towns in the Valley as their base for security and cultural solidarity. They had significant economic leverage and used it to their advantage to achieve a remarkable level of prosperity despite the forces arrayed against them, until the demographic implications of the 1882 Chinese Exclusion Act and the 1892 Geary Act became too much to overcome, alongside the arrival of a viable replacement labor force around 1900.

The building of the First Transcontinental Railroad brought large numbers of Chinese laborers to the United States. In 1865, the Central Pacific Railroad headed by the "Big Four"—Leland Stanford, Charles Crocker, Collis Huntington and Timothy Hopkins—hired Chinese throughout California and, needing thousands more, recruited from villages in southern China. More than twelve thousand Chinese laborers were employed in building the rugged 690-mile route to Promontory, Utah, to join the Union Pacific, uniting the country by rail. The Chinese accomplished the impossible, building fifteen tunnels in the Sierra Nevada Mountains and laying ten miles of track in one day. Charles Crocker stated before the Senate Committee investigating Chinese immigration:

> *They are equal to the best of white men. We tested that in the Summit Tunnel, which is the hardest granite...*
>
> *The Chinese were skilled in using the hammer and the drill; and they proved themselves equal to the very best Cornish miners in that work. They are very trusty, they are very intelligent, and they live up to their contracts.*
>
> *...today if I had a big job of work that I wanted to do quick with, and had a limited time to do it in, I would take Chinese labor to do it with, because of its greater reliability and steadiness, and their aptitude and capacity for hard work.*[3]

After the transcontinental railroad was completed on May 10, 1869, thousands of Chinese went to seek other jobs. Some worked on other railroad lines, some went to the Sacramento delta to build levees and many were needed as agricultural workers in the great valleys of California. In the Napa Valley, they found work in the hop fields and vineyards, where they used their skills in building wine caves. Their contributions to the transcontinental railroad, the greatest engineering feat of the nineteenth century, were too often erased from history. They lived and worked in peril as they became scapegoats for economic woes of the 1870s, with groups such as the Order of the Caucasians giving rise to the vociferous and powerful Workingmen's Party. "The Chinese Must Go" was the rallying cry of the labor movement in the 1870s.

Politicians joined in condemning the Chinese, accusing them of being a degraded people and a moral threat to American society and Chinatowns a public nuisance. Chinese immigration became the major political issue of California, resulting in a milestone federal law, the Chinese Exclusion Act of 1882, which suspended the immigration of Chinese laborers for ten years and prohibited Chinese people from becoming U.S. citizens. Made permanent in 1902, the act of Congress institutionalized discrimination against Chinese, emboldened racist groups, incited expulsions of Chinese and prompted the violent destruction of Chinatowns throughout the West. Chinese were made perpetual aliens and denied life, liberty and the pursuit of happiness. There was a Chinese saying at the time: "There are three businesses open to us Chinese—the restaurant business, the laundry business and the gambling business."

The Napa Valley experience is particularly interesting because the Chinese were there at the very beginning of the wine industry, as well as the early days of quicksilver mining, hop farming and leather tanning. Moreover, they provided the only possible source of labor that could have made any of those industries successful in those crucial early decades. Yet xenophobic locals and anti-Chinese immigration policies at the state and federal levels eventually drove the Chinese out in favor of other labor groups, such as the more socially acceptable white Italian working class.[4] Those Chinese contributions are largely forgotten. Today, there are numerous wineries with Italian names and roots, yet there are almost no wineries, places or monuments acknowledging and explaining the significant Chinese presence or contributions.[5]

An illustrated history of Napa County, written in 1878, describes the Napa Valley, an area bursting with beauty and opportunity:

> *The wheat fields and vineyards of Napa spread out in beautiful contrast on the landscape, and elegant and costly homes adorn eminences and pretty*

values. The vine and fig tree mark the settler's home. Curative waters are found in various localities. Not only the soil but the air administers to the wealth of the resident, Living streams flow in every direction. Neither blight nor failure visit Napa valley [sic], *but plenty, peace and prosperity seem to be the lot of the residents of this favored spot in California.*

The business of raising grapes and making them into wine is already a very great one in California, and Napa County now has the name of producing the best wines in the State. It has precisely the soil required for the different varieties. The gravelly valleys and plains, or the more elevated hillsides and warm slopes.[6]

There are three significant towns in the Napa Valley that I will focus on in this book: the largest town of Napa at the southern end, the agricultural town of St. Helena in the middle of the valley and the resort town of Calistoga at the northern tip.[7] There are also smaller towns of Yountville, Rutherford and Oakville that fill in gaps between the larger towns.

Unfortunately, primary sources from the Chinese laborers themselves who worked in the Napa Valley during this period are practically nonexistent. Many Chinese immigrants could read, as demonstrated by at least twenty Chinese-language newspapers that were in operation in the late nineteenth century, mostly around San Francisco.[8] Yet we don't have any surviving documents from local Chinese workers. We do have oral histories from some families, like those of Jue Joe and Chan Wah Jack, that help fill in some gaps. In addition, there are contemporaneous accounts that can be informative, if read with a skeptical eye toward their anti-Chinese bias. Over the thirty-year period in question, local newspapers had hundreds of articles, editorials, letters to the editor and advertisements addressing Chinese laborers, their local Chinatowns and the issues townspeople had with the local Chinese community. This was an area of intense local interest at the time.

The Chinese immigrant workers were made scapegoats for every social and economic ill affecting society. Newspapers across the country, including those in the Napa Valley, reported Chinese in a negative light. It was national policy to denigrate the Chinese. Cartoons in the newspapers and journals, showing villainous caricatures of Chinese, perpetuated stereotypes that lasted more than a century. The newspaper articles of the time used derogatory terms for Chinese people that are clearly offensive and unacceptable today. Almost every article that referred to Chinese residents that I use in this book contains derisive terms like "Chinamen," "Coolies," "Mongolians," "Celestials" or "Johns." I have included the text of these articles as written

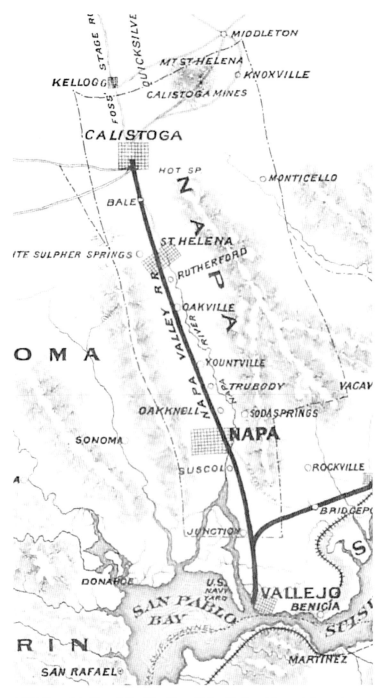

1878 *Map of the Napa Valley*. The Napa Valley Railroad formed the main transportation link that ran up and down the Valley. *From* Illustrations of Napa County, California: With Historical Sketch.

because it is important to hear and understand how Chinese people were called at the time to dehumanize them. In every case, these terms are within quotes, and their original source is referenced. This was not unique to the Napa Valley and was common in California and across the United States, but it doesn't make the terminology excusable.

During the Gilded Age and the Progressive Era in U.S. history (1860s through the early 1900s), more than 40 million immigrants came to America from Europe, Latin America and Asia to help transform the United States into an economic powerhouse.[9] This influx of immigrants also brought intense and blatant racial discrimination from every level of government and throughout society. No group suffered as much from those anti-immigration forces as the Chinese, who were the first group to be denied immigration and citizenship in the United States solely based on their race.[10] The level of success the Chinese had in the Napa Valley is remarkable given these headwinds. Their story is one of a strong entrepreneurial spirit and tenacity that should not be forgotten. This book will tell a comprehensive account of how the Chinese helped, in their own way, transform a small rural community in California into an area of worldwide renown and economic dominance.

Chapter 1

ARRIVAL

The Opium Wars, the Taiping Rebellion, secret society uprisings and clan warfare had devastating consequences for laborers and peasants in China in the latter half of the 1800s. Competition from foreign markets, increased taxes, growing population, land scarcity and unrest due to local uprisings all contributed to a mass emigration movement. One estimate suggests that 2.5 million Chinese departed the mainland to other countries around the world between 1840 and 1900.[11] Some emigrants from China left voluntarily, while some were taken against their will. Chinese people who left freely either paid for their tickets or got passage in exchange for payment when they reached their destinations. This group tended to go to California or Australia. Unfree "coolie" laborers, who were abducted, were shipped to places like Peru or Cuba to work plantations that no longer had the labor of African slaves.[12] Consequently, most California arrivals from China were highly motivated, entrepreneurial and either able to pay for passage themselves or were confident in their ability to reimburse passage once they arrived.

Anti-Chinese sentiment in California was present from the beginning of large-scale emigration from China. The major draw for Chinese immigrating to California was the prospect of gold. Between 1848 and 1867, more than 70 percent of all Chinese immigrants to the United States settled in California, where mining dominated the economy.[13] Even though gold was discovered in California in 1849, the first significant Chinese immigration wave of twenty thousand did not arrive until 1852.

The Pacific Mail steamer the *Great Republic* was one of four steamships traveling between China and the United States in 1874. *From lithograph by Charles Parsons, 1867.*

Unfortunately for the Chinese, by the time of their arrival, the era of the individual gold miner striking it rich on easily accessed surface mines was ending. Through hard work and determination, they were able to eke out a living for much of the 1850s and 1860s. The American and European miners resented even this modest success of the Chinese miners and began one of the first sustained anti-Chinese labor movements in California.[14] Chinese immigrants continued to arrive in significant numbers to California; sixteen thousand arrived in 1854, and then between two and eight thousand arrived each year until 1868.[15]

By the early 1870s, Chinese labor was pervasive throughout California. Charles Nordoff, an East Coast journalist, wrote an eyewitness account of what he saw regarding "John Chinaman" as he traveled throughout the state:

> *John now does most of the washing and ironing all over California; "Woo-gung," or "Ah Lee" or "Fooh Lien," "Washing and Ironing done"—with sometimes the addition "Buttons sewed on strong" is the sign you see oftenest in California towns. In the cities he collects the garbage; he is cook and waiter; he makes the cigars; he works in the woolen mills; go into any manufacturing place and you will see his face; there is a Chinaman and a half on every mile of the Central Pacific Railroad; he raises two-thirds of the vegetables consumed in the State; he makes a good shepherd; in the farming districts the commonest sight is to see John driving a wagon, or ploughing; the lonely ranch-man keeps a Chinese cook; hundreds of Chinese*

are going over the old mining "slum," and making money by his patient toil;
he keeps his New-year's week with jollity and fire-crackers, from San Diego
to Sacramento; and so far east as Denver, in Colorado, you see his sign,
"Lo Wing, Washing and Ironing." Both political parties in California
denounce the Chinaman on their platforms; but if you go to the houses of
the men who made these platforms, you will find Chinese servants; if you
visit their farms or ranches, you will find Chinese hands; and if you ask the
political leader, after dinner what he really thinks, he will tell you that he
could not get on without Chinese, and that the cry against them is the most
abominable demagogism; all of which is true.[16]

Commercial agricultural work in California prior to the 1870s was
performed primarily by Native Americans and then by cast-off gold miners.
In the early 1800s, the Franciscan padres who built missions up and down
the California coast established teams of farmworkers made up mostly of
Native Americans. These workers would either toil on large farms owned by
the missions or work as contract laborers for other farms around California.
They were ostensibly under the protection and religious instruction of the
Franciscans, but the native farmworkers were managed under a "rigid system
of unremitting supervision" that made them "worse than slaves."[17]

By the 1850s, the Native American population had declined dramatically
due to various "Indian Wars" carried out by local governors, relocation to
numerous reservations and self-selecting out of the brutal work as an indentured
farmworker.[18] In the 1850s and 1860s, many failed gold and silver miners had
no choice but to turn to agricultural work. They were the first truly migrant
farmworkers in California and were called "bindlemen" because they carried
a "bindle," or bundle, consisting of a canvas blanket rolled tightly around their
few possessions and slung over the shoulders as they moved from farm to farm.
These bindlemen were mostly white Europeans but also included Chilean
peasants, among others, who came to California for the opportunity to strike
it rich in the gold and silver mines.[19] Bindlemen were an independent and
hardworking, yet hard-carousing, group. The arrival of Chinese laborers in
the 1850s and 1860s, some of whom turned to farm work, brought a different
kind of worker. They had a reputation of being compliant and reliable. In a
widely read article in the March 1869 issue of *Overland Monthly* titled "How
Our Chinamen Are Employed," it stated:

On many ranches all the laborers are people whose muscles were hardened on
their little farms in China, and who there learned those lessons of industry,

patience, and economy which render them of incalculable service for those who, in this country, see fit to employ them. With but little instruction they learn to manage the teams, to run the machinery, and to perform all the labor needed upon a farm.[20]

Agriculture had been considered a big business enterprise in California as soon as it became a state in 1848 and white settlers arrived in large numbers in the 1850s. Farmers in California, geographically very distant from traditional sources of credit on the East Coast or Europe, paid a high price for access to capital, as well as extremely high transportation and marketing costs. This confluence of large farms, large labor requirements, high capital costs and high freight costs put enormous pressure on farmers throughout California to keep the cost of labor down.[21] Chinese laborers, who had to settle for lower wages than any other group—as they were legally unable to work in many traditional jobs in the state, such as the government or corporations—were a logical source of labor for many large land owners.

The labor needs of the vineyard owners in the Napa Valley made the 1870s a transformative decade for the Chinese workforce. The American Civil War in the 1860s had disrupted trade from the East Coast and Europe and gave a chance for the local wine industry to establish itself and grow through the early 1870s. The Chinese laborers would work for just $1.00 per day and provide their own food and cooking—significantly less than the $1.50 daily rate for white labor.[22] Vineyard work required large amounts of labor for only a few critical months a year during planting and harvesting seasons. The Chinese workers were organized into labor gangs that could be called on at a moment's notice to meet this need. This approach was established early in the Napa Valley when Chinese laborers could be called up quickly from San Francisco to work the vineyard harvest.

As Napa Valley wine sales were starting to significantly increase in the late 1870s, a blight called Phylloxera was decimating the vineyards of France, and the Napa Valley wine industry knew that it had a golden opportunity. As reported in the *St. Helena Star* in late 1879, "The destruction of the French vineyards is a fixed fact. The eyes of the world will be turned to our valleys in tremendous hope and anticipation of good wine."[23] The vineyard owners went on a massive planting spree, further driving up demand for labor, which could only be satisfied by one group: Chinese workers.[24] These Chinese immigrants benefited from the high demand for their labor, but they had to contend with the corresponding rise of anti-Chinese sentiment in the Napa Valley. They were relentlessly discriminated against, yet they were able to create a supportive community that remained a significant presence in the Valley for decades.

The population of Napa County expanded rapidly between 1860 and 1890 before leveling off in 1900. The Chinese population increased more than tenfold between 1860 and 1870 and then more than tripled between 1870 and 1880. This rapid rise of the Chinese population in Napa County, both in absolute and relative terms, undoubtedly gave the white residents, many of whom were already prejudiced against Chinese people, anxiety. The Chinese population gradually declined from 1880 to 1900—an unsurprising trend given the passage of the Federal 1882 Chinese Exclusion Act, which prohibited immigration of laborers from China, as well as subsequent anti-immigration laws at the federal level.

TABLE 1. POPULATION OF CHINESE RESIDENTS IN NAPA COUNTY, 1860–1900.

	1860	*1870*	*1880*	*1890*	*1900*
White	5,448	6,725	12,160	15,426	15,857
Chinese	17	263	907	875	541
Ratio	3	39	75	57	34
% Change		1,200%	92%	-24%	-40%

Ratio is the number of Chinese residents per 1,000 white residents. % change is the change in ratio from one decade to the next. Even at its height, the Chinese population of Napa County never exceeded seven percent of the total population.[25]

THE STORY OF JUE JOE, ASPARAGUS KING

Jue Joe would be considered a remarkable man in any circumstance, given his very humble origins and his subsequent accomplishments.[26] However, what makes Jue Joe particularly special to us is that he was a Chinese immigrant who worked as an agricultural laborer in the Napa Valley between 1878 and 1886, and we happen to know quite a bit of his life story after he left the vineyards.

Jue Joe (born into the Zhao clan) was born in China in 1856. His family was very poor, and they worked in a chicken coop in Guangzhou, Guangdong

Sketch of Chinese immigrants on the way to San Francisco on the Pacific Mail steamship *Alaska. From* Harper's Weekly, *May 20, 1876.*

Province, China. Growing up, he vowed that his descendants would never suffer as he had. In 1874, at the age of eighteen, he sailed alone to California by working as a cabin boy and jumped ship in San Francisco. His mother sent him off with sixteen pounds of rice to eat during the voyage—when he arrived in San Francisco, he had just a quarter pound left.

Once in San Francisco, he sought out the Chinese Consolidated Benevolent Association, better known as the Chinese Six Companies. It provided a variety of services to newly arrived Chinese immigrants, and most importantly for Jue Joe, it helped new immigrants find employment.[27] The association found him work in the vineyards, first in Marysville (near Sacramento) from 1874 to 1878 and then in St. Helena in the Napa Valley from 1878 to 1886. His original wage was fifty cents per day for his work in Marysville.

Jue Joe had a streak of independence and liked to do things his own way. He always wore a khaki shirt, khaki pants and knee-high boots. When working on a ranch, he would walk around with a Colt .45 strapped in a holster, which he would fire once per year to clean it out. He slept with a knife under his pillow so he would be ready in case anything unexpected happened.

In 1882 or 1883, Jue Joe obtained his first certificate of identity in St. Helena in response to the 1882 Chinese Exclusion Act. This was an important step in the wake of that legislation because if he were to go back to China and then return to the United States, he would need that identification. Of all immigrant groups, only Chinese workers needed to prove that they belonged in the United States. There was a significant rise of anti-Chinese (called "Anti-Coolie" at the time) sentiment, organization and even violence in the mid-1880s in St. Helena. Jue Joe suffered an injury in anti-Chinese riots. His later immigration papers noted a gash at the end of his right eyebrow and a crooked little finger on his left hand. Jue Joe told his son San Tong of attacks he had received at the hands of "nogooders" when he was a young man working the vineyards of Northern California. As a Chinese immigrant with very limited rights, he could not fight back. In 1886, he left St. Helena due to the rising anti-Chinese sentiment. In the same year, an anti-Chinese mob marched to St. Helena's Chinatown and demanded that everyone vacate within ten days or face serious consequences.

Jue Joe got work laying tracks for the Southern Pacific Railroad from a Chinese labor broker in Oakland's railroad yard. His wage was one dollar per day. From 1887 to 1893, Jue Joe was employed as a laborer on the railroad and eventually ended up in Los Angeles. In 1896, Jue Joe leased a farm and grew potatoes in Chatsworth, where he sold them at a produce market in Los Angeles and became quite successful. Six years later, Jue Joe returned to China and left his business with his brother Jue Shee. Jue Joe married Leong Shee in an arranged marriage, built a house and began to farm in China.

Unfortunately, his brother suffered business losses in the United States, and in 1906, Jue Joe decided to move back to Los Angeles to remake his fortune. He left Leong Shee in China with his two sons. Twelve years later, he sent for his family, and they emigrated from China to the United States. Jue Joe was allowed to bring his family over because of a loophole in the Chinese Exclusion Act allowing merchants and their families to immigrate.

In the 1920s, Jue Joe and Leong Shee had two daughters, and he continued to expand his farming operations in Southern California. By 1934, Jue Joe's asparagus farms had become very successful, and he was hailed as the "Asparagus King" by the *Los Angeles Times*. In 1941, Jue Joe passed away and had to transfer all his family landholdings to his American-born daughters, since native-born Chinese, like his sons, could not hold land in the United States at that time.

Jue Joe's story of discrimination, achievement, setbacks, perseverance and eventual success is the embodiment of the American Dream. It started

Jue Joe; his wife, Leong Shee; his two sons who were born in China; and his two daughters who were born in the United States. *From collection of Jack Jue, Joe's great-grandson.*

with travel to a better life in California and hard physical labor in the vineyards of Napa Valley. Many of the Chinese individuals in this book persevered through equally challenging circumstances. While we may not know many of their stories, their contributions to the Napa Valley, California and the United States should not be forgotten. It is remarkable that they achieved as much as they did given the tremendous challenges men like Jue Joe had to overcome.

Chapter 2

RURAL NAPA VALLEY

hinese workers provided the labor force that drove many of the emerging industries in the Napa Valley in the late nineteenth century. Not only were they an available labor pool, but they were also willing to work for cheaper wages than white laborers and work at jobs that were considered dangerous or "beneath the dignity" of white laborers. As Herbert Howe Bancroft wrote in 1890:

> For twenty years Chinese labor has acted as a protective tariff, enabling California to establish wealth-creating industries, which form the basis of her present and future greatness; and it would be about as sensible to drive out all steam-engines or other machinery as for this reason alone to drive out the Chinese.[28]

The general occupation of "laborer" was the most common profession self-reported by Chinese workers in both the 1870 and 1880 federal censuses (see Tables 5 and 6 in the appendix.) This could encompass a wide range of activities, but it mostly referred to various outdoor manual labor jobs. Chinese workers were the dominant labor force in the vineyards, hop fields and local railroad construction and maintenance. They were involved in quicksilver mining, general farming and building roads and bridges.

In just the ten years between 1870 and 1880, there was a significant increase in the Chinese population of the Napa Valley and the diversification of the jobs they performed. Some of the diversity may have been due to more accurate census recordkeeping, but this was a significant growth period for

Napa Valley, so that is consistent with new and expanding kinds of jobs for everyone, including Chinese workers.[29]

VITICULTURE

Robert Louis Stevenson wrote about the early days of the Napa Valley wine industry in his 1873 book, *Silverado Squatters*. His famous quote, "and the wine is bottled poetry," adorns the large welcome signs that greet visitors today when they visit the Napa Valley. The more complete quote accurately describes the speculative nature of viticulture in the Valley between 1870 and 1900. It was a hit-or-miss operation, and economic success was in no way guaranteed. It is unsurprising that many vineyard owners would want to tightly control expenses, especially one of the highest-cost items: labor. Stevenson's full quote is as follows:

> *Wine in California is still in the experimental stage; and when you taste a vintage, grave economical questions are involved. The beginning of vine-planting is like the beginning of mining for the precious metals: the wine-grower also "Prospects." One corner of land after another is tried with one kind of grape after another. This is a failure; that is better; a third best. So, bit by bit, they grope about for their Clos Vougeot and Lafite. Those lodes and pockets of earth, more precious than the precious ores, that yield inimitable fragrance and soft fire; those virtuous Bonanzas, where the soil has sublimated under sun and stars to something finer, and the wine is bottled poetry.*[30]

Chinese laborers made up the vast majority of vineyard workers throughout the Napa Valley in the late nineteenth century and were indispensable in the development of the early wine industry. As early as 1873, Charles Menefee, who wrote about daily life in Napa County, said, "One of the most important questions presented to the agriculturist is that of labor. The farmers frequently find it impossible to get laborers to perform their work. A great portion of the labor employed during the vintage in picking and shipping grapes is Chinese."[31] By the 1880s, they composed up to 80 percent of the labor force working in vineyards.[32] They were immigrants from Canton and came from villages where generation after generation plowed the same fields and planted the same crops, usually rice and a variety of vegetables. They would have been familiar with making rice wine and brandy, but wine from grapes would have been new to them. While they learned quickly about how to cultivate and harvest a crop that was not native to their land, they would have consumed rice wine instead of locally produced wines they helped harvest.

There were many reasons why Chinese laborers competed successfully with white laborers in getting work. The most important reason was that they were significantly less expensive compared with white labor alternatives. Charles Krug, owner of a large vineyard, said that he paid Chinese workers $1.00 per day and did not feed or house them on site, while he had to pay white workers $1.00 a day in addition to room and board or $1.50 per day without room and board.[33] Each day during harvest season, the Chinese laborer picked an average of 1,500 pounds of grapes for their dollar.[34] In addition, Chinese workers had a reputation of being extremely reliable. If they entered into a contract to do a job, they completed that contract. A California labor contractor as early as 1869 said that he had dealings with at least twenty-five thousand Chinese railroad workers and "never knew a single case where a Chinaman has broken his contract."[35] One of the intractable labor problems in the Napa Valley in the 1870s, as it was throughout the state, was that the white laborer was considered unreliable. They had the reputation of abandoning their tools in the middle of a vineyard and heading to the California foothills whenever news of a new gold or silver strike reached town. Chinese workers rarely left the fields to join their fellow laborers in pursuit of riches because they took pride in fulfilling their labor arrangements.[36] Vineyard owners praised Chinese workers for their general steadiness and for not drinking on the job.[37]

Chinese workers had a more varied diet than white laborers and may have been healthier overall. Chinese workers in agricultural fields drank cold tea that was brought to them in the field during breaks. This tea was made with boiled water, which would have been safer to use than non-boiled water consumed by other laborers. Most of the food they ate came from China and was available in Chinese stores throughout the West. A typical daily ration for a Chinese railroad worker was two pounds of rice; one pound of fish, beef or pork; tea; and a variety of vegetables. Examples of the variety of foods available for purchase by Chinese railroad workers include dried oysters, dried fish, sweet rice crackers, dried bamboo sprouts, four kinds of dried fruits, five kinds of dried vegetables, Chinese bacon, mushrooms, tea and rice.[38]

Finally, there was a cultural aversion to working in vineyards by some white laborers. In the early decades of vineyard planting, vines were planted

Chinese laborers working in a California vineyard. Note that workers must stoop over to prune the vines. *From the Huntington Digital Library Collection of Charles C Pierce.*

such that the grapes grew about eighteen inches off the ground. To properly harvest the grapes, laborers had to spend their days in the baking sun bent over at the waist. White laborers called this "stoop labor" and considered it demeaning. The willingness of the Chinese laborers to do this work was not understood as a superior work ethic, but rather was portrayed in patronizing racial terms. The *San Francisco Wine Merchant* reported that "the best hand in the grape field by all odds is the little Chinaman. He grows close to the ground, so does not have to bend his back like a large, white man."[39]

Owners of small vineyards who only needed a few extra laborers around harvest time had the option of using white laborers. Owners of large vineyards, however, had no choice but turn to Chinese labor. This had been an issue in the Napa Valley as early as 1872. At a St. Helena meeting of principle agricultural owners, called the Farmers' Club, the men discussed what could be done about Chinese labor given the shortage of workers on their farms and fields. They questioned whether labor rates of Chinese workers should be regulated so they wouldn't undercut white labor rates or whether it should be left to the free market to decide. Some argued that while the Chinese are supposed to be inferior, if "their knowledge and skill exceed ours—if their civilization is better than ours—then they deserve to win." One farmer suggested that if they could not hire enough white laborers, the "only remain'g [*sic*] remedy is to cultivate home industry—to make the labor of our children available." He had done this on his own farm and found it "more pleasant and more profitable." Despite their complaining, none of the vineyard owners likely believed that child labor would solve their problem. Chinese laborers remained the only viable economical solution.

St. Helena's Charles Krug, who even by 1872 had significant experience with Chinese workers on his vineyards, defended the use of Chinese workers. He said that he would have preferred to use white labor but had no choice but to turn to Chinese labor. He said they "do pretty well—never too much raunch [*sic*]," and some of them had been in his employ for three to five years. Dr. B.K. Rule had a similar experience to Krug on his winery. He said that he employed a "first-class" white man to supervise the Chinese workers and then "threw all the responsibility on him." At the end of the meeting, they all agreed that while white labor was preferable to Chinese labor, nothing could be done about it but pay the good Chinese workers the wages they wanted.[40]

This issue became increasingly problematic as the demand for labor skyrocketed due to the massive vineyard plantings in the 1880s. The demographics of the agricultural labor pool was changing rapidly. As the Farmers' Club members discussed, many vineyard owners still strongly preferred white laborers, and some worked on most vineyards in some capacity. But there were just not enough willing to do the work to meet the demand.[41] Menefee commented that the vineyard owners "are not favorably disposed to these Asiatics, but often find themselves reduced to the necessities of accepting these or none."[42]

The Chinese vineyard workers eventually realized that their dominant labor position meant they had economic power relative to the owners who employed them. Chinese labor immigration was curtailed after 1882 due to the Chinese Exclusion Act. Alternate sources of labor were in short supply, and vineyard acres under cultivation continued to grow. Between 1880 and 1886, the number of wineries grew from 48 to 175, and wine production grew from 2,910,700 gallons to 4,800,000 gallons.[43] By 1887, the *St. Helena Star* was regularly reporting on the shortage of labor across the Valley. White laborers were getting $2.00 a day, and Chinese laborers, who were getting $1.25 per day, successfully went on strike at the end of September for a 20 percent increase to $1.50 per day.[44] This was a significant development and demonstrated a level of coordination, organization and, most importantly, empowerment among the Chinese labor force. This reflected a broader trend of Chinese agricultural laborers going on strike for higher wages throughout the 1880s in different parts of California as they realized their domination of certain farming labor markets gave them leverage.[45] Although their political rights had not improved in the 1880s, the economic outlook of the Chinese laborers had improved considerably. This was a dramatic reversal from a labor group that was frequently stereotyped as "docile" and would not go on strike.

There was significant concern about what would happen to the wine industry if acres under cultivation continued to expand and there were not enough Chinese labor to work the vines. E.W. Hilgard, writing in the *Overland Monthly* in 1884, said that in addition to ensuring Phylloxera did not overwhelm local vineyards, the other "threatening difficulty is that of a scarcity of labor, and for the immediate future it is certainly a serious one. The exclusion act is rapidly rendering Chinese labor unavailable, and no other as yet appears to take its place. The difficulty is especially serious in the case of the great vineyard enterprises covering thousands of acres." He drew an analogy that local vineyard owners were "in nearly the same predicament as were the cotton-planters of the South after the war, when they found themselves unable to command the negro labor that had previously run their thousand-acre plantations so smoothly."[46] While he wished for more Chinese laborers to be available in California because they were good workers, he was not being altruistic. Other commentators would tout the Chinese work ethic in California while simultaneously denigrating them. As Francis Sheldon, writing in the *Overland Monthly*, argued in 1886:

> *It is the insidiousness of the Chinese method that is its most dangerous feature. They come upon us so quietly, and so quickly appropriate places for themselves, that it is too late when we awake to the damage that is done. It matters not that their feeling is friendly toward us. The gist of the matter—that which makes their unlimited coming an invasion—lies in the fact that they have the ability within themselves to out-compete us in any and all branches of industry in which we engage.*[47]

Even though the vineyard owners reluctantly admitted that they needed Chinese labor to be successful, they went to great pains to hide the fact from the outside world. As Napa Valley wines began to gain a reputation for taste and quality, the vintners did not want anything damaging that impression. They worried that if it became common knowledge that Chinese laborers

"The Vintage in California—At Work at the Wine Presses." *From* Harper's Weekly, *October 5, 1878.*

were working the vineyards, it would raise questions about cleanliness and the possibility of foreign diseases. In 1887, *Harper's Weekly* published a lengthy article titled "The Vintage in California" that focused on Sonoma and Napa Valley wines. As part of the article, the periodical commissioned an artist, Paul Frenzeny, to do a pencil sketch of a winemaking scene. He took artistic license and transformed a scene of Chinese in the field picking grapes to be one of them stomping grapes with their bare feet—a process the technologically advanced vintners had abandoned years prior. When the picture was printed in the October 5, 1878 issue titled "The Vintage in California—At Work at the Wine Presses" alongside the article, it caused widespread dismay for local vineyard owners and, as they feared, brought out strong anti-Chinese sentiment from across the state and nation. Despite threats and even occasional violence against their property or the Chinese workers themselves, the vineyard owners persevered and kept employing the laborers. While the vineyard owners may have chosen to keep the Chinese working in the vineyard despite public pressure, it is worth noting that this incident helped the California white labor organizations justify a blatantly anti-Chinese article in the 1879 California Constitution.[48]

One argument that was frequently put forth was that if Chinese labor were necessary for large vineyards to succeed, the answer might be to renounce large vineyards in favor of smaller ones that could use family and a few white laborers to bring in the crop. An article in the July 9, 1884 *St. Helena Star* argued that Napa Valley vintners should pay for immigrants from France, Germany and Italy to come to work on the vineyards. If that did not work, then "in a nutshell this: Have smaller vineyards, more of them and do the work ourselves. A growing and valuable industry would be retarded, but it will live."[49] Despite this call to action, none of the vineyard owners showed any interest in deconstructing their profitable large vineyards in favor of poorer, racially homogenous and smaller ones. Chinese vineyard workers were there to stay until labor demand shrank or until vineyard owners could find economically viable alternatives.

SPOTLIGHT ON SCHRAMSBERG VINEYARDS

One of the few places in the Napa Valley where you can still see direct evidence of the labor of Chinese workers on a winery is at Schramsberg Vineyards. In 1862, Jacob Schram purchased a two-hundred-acre property on the hillside of Mount Diamond between present-day St. Helena and Calistoga and began development of one of the first hillside vineyards in the Napa Valley. In 1870, the grapes were ready for harvest, and Schram decided to construct a set of wine caves dug back into the mountain itself to provide a consistently cool and environmentally stable location for the wine to age. Digging caves into the side of a mountain was labor-intensive work. Many Chinese laborers were just coming off jobs on the transcontinental railroad and the Napa Valley Railroad and were available to do the backbreaking and dangerous work of excavating the caves. Many of them had experience with explosives during the building of the transcontinental railroad when they had to blast a path through the Sierra Nevada Mountain range. Even with the aid of dynamite, however, it still required hard work with picks and shovels to construct the caves.

The Chinese labor gangs worked quickly and took about a year to blast, dig and shape the first set of caves. Overall, they dug a subterranean complex about one-quarter mile in length into the mountainside. These caves, still in use today, are about seven feet tall and are roughly cylindrical in shape.

After the caves were dug, Chinese laborers continued to work at the winery doing a wide variety of jobs. The winery is set back almost two miles from the main north–south travel route in the Valley, so they would have had no choice but to both live and work on the property. They harvested the

Above: Wine caves dug by Chinese laborers at Schramsberg Winery are still in use today. *Author's collection.*

Right: Narrow tunnels connect larger rooms within the wine caves. *Author's collection.*

Left: Cook for Jacob Schram of the Schramsberg Winery. Image predates 1905. *Courtesy of Schramsberg Winery archives.*

Below: Winery employees posing in front of the Schram Mansion at the Schramsberg. Note the one Chinese worker posing on the left. *Courtesy of Schramsberg Winery archives.*

The "Chinese Bunkhouse" on the property at Schramsberg that used to house Chinese workers. *Author's collection.*

grapes, did chores about the winery and homestead and worked as domestic servants for the Schrams.

There is a building on the property known as the "Chinese Bunkhouse" where the Chinese field laborers and domestic servants were housed on site. Inside the bunkhouse, there are two rooms; each has a door to the outside, and there is an inside opening connecting the two rooms. The bigger room consists of a large fireplace that was used for both heating and cooking. The wooden rafters on the inside of the roof still are coated black from the frequent cooking fires. The smaller room consists of storage shelves and may have been used as a sleeping area.[50]

By 1881, the winery was operating close to capacity, and it had produced 87,237 cases of wine since it first opened. Jacob Schram decided that it was time to build a second set of tunnels to allow him to age and bottle more wine at one time. This set of tunnels was also constructed by Chinese laborers. The second set of caves is much more extensive than the first. Not only are they taller and wider than the initial set of caves—they are at least ten feet tall compared to the original seven—but they are also much longer and more complex. These caves took longer to construct than the first set—well over a year—but since Schram already had one set of caves in operation, he was able to take more time with the new set of caves and ensure that they were large enough to accommodate future winery operations. Today, the inside of the first set of caves has been sprayed with a concrete sealant to

Left: The second phase of cave construction at Schramsberg had larger cave openings. Instead of barrels, thousands of bottles are stored in this section. *Author's collection.*

Below: Pick marks left by the Chinese laborers during the 1881 wine cave construction. *Author's collection.*

keep out moisture, but the second set of caves looks much like it was when it was originally constructed. It is possible to still see the pick marks from the Chinese laborers where they dug out the caves, at least partially by hand.[51]

Interestingly, Schramsberg sparkling wines have played a part in the more modern history between China and the United States as well. Richard Nixon visited China in 1972 in a historic trip to reestablish diplomatic relations between the United States and China. On February 25, 1972, in the middle of the trip, Richard Nixon gave a famous "Toast to Peace" at a state dinner hosted by Chinese premier Zhou Enlai. As Barbara Walters reported, the toast was made with a 1969 vintage Schramsberg "Blanc de Blancs" sparkling wine. It was the first time a California wine was served on the international stage by a U.S. president.[52]

Hop Farming

Grapes were not the only crop grown in the Napa Valley that was destined for alcoholic beverages. Hops, critical for brewing beer, was the second in crop yield behind only grapes. In addition to beer, hops were also used in baking and in the production of medicines. It was mostly grown for export, as England in the late nineteenth century consumed as many hops as the rest of the world combined. The fortunes of hop yards rose and fell considerably each year depending on the weather and worldwide supply and demand, especially from Europe. The hops were trained to grow up wooden poles and required about 1,500 poles per acre that was fully planted. The cost for poles for a fifteen-acre hop yard was about $1,100, which was a significant investment. Picking of the hops was "done chiefly by Chinamen and it takes a force of fifty about a month to pick a 15-acre field." In addition to the planting, growing and picking of hops, they had to be dried, cured and baled. The high capital and labor expense of growing hops made it a perilous business.[53]

Unlike vineyards, which were present up and down the Valley, hops were only grown in St. Helena. The first hop field in Napa County was planted by Mr. A. Clock in 1868. By 1876, there were a total of four hop farms around St. Helena: Clock's, R.F. Montgomery's, Charles A. Storey's and James Dowdell's.[54] Mr. Clock's hops were so well known that he was awarded the title of "Champion Hop-Grower of the World" at the 1876 Centennial Exposition in Philadelphia.[55]

An 1878 sketch of a hop farm in St. Helena showing Chinese farmers in the field. Chinese composed 100 percent of hop farm labor in the county. *From* Illustrations of Napa County, California: With Historical Sketch.

In 1870, the single largest occupation of Chinese, other than the generic "laborer" occupation, was working in the hop fields. By 1880, eleven thousand pounds of hops were harvested each year across the entire county.[56] The *Napa County Reporter* said that hops selling at seven or eight cents per pound in 1879 were selling at forty or fifty cents per pound just three years later.[57] Hop farmers and vineyard owners had similar problems getting inexpensive labor to work on their fields. In 1876, hop yard owner Charles A. Storey employed a labor gang of sixty Chinese laborers to harvest the hops on his property.[58] Unlike vineyard workers, which consisted of both Chinese and white workers, hop picking in the Napa Valley was exclusively done by Chinese laborers. In 1884, the five hop farms in the county employed a total of 335 Chinese laborers to harvest the crop.[59]

The *St. Helena Star* grumbled that hop yards around the nearby town of Healdsburg in Sonoma County employed about one thousand hop pickers and that they were all white men, women and children, yet the Napa Valley farmers only used Chinese labor.[60] The *Star* was so disgusted with the prevalence of Chinese laborers on the hop field that the following year, it reported that an agent was in nearby Sonoma and Mendocino Counties arranging for African American laborers to be imported from the South to work in the hop fields there. The paper editorialized that importing African American laborers to the Napa Valley to work in the vineyards and hop yards would be a considerable improvement over the Chinese hop pickers.[61]

Just as their vineyard worker counterparts had done, Chinese hop pickers went on strike demanding a raise in pay in 1887. They were getting $1.00 per day and struck for $1.25 per day. This incensed local farmers, who redoubled their efforts to recruit white laborers to work the fields. James Dowdell, the most vocal St. Helena hop farmer, said that the nearby community of Healdsburg had recently swapped out Chinese labor for white laborers and that it "worked well." He noted that since it was harvest time in the hop field, he could not switch out his Chinese laborers this season, but he was "willing to fix up temporary accommodations and give white labor a show if it can be obtained."[62] Apparently, he did not believe that white laborers would be willing to camp out in the fields at night during harvest, even though he forced his Chinese workers to do that every season.

Dowdell was unsuccessful with his plan for better accommodations to attract white labor, but that did not deter him. In 1892, he decided to involve the entire St. Helena community in his effort to recruit white laborers. He offered prizes to all townspeople, including married women and single boys and girls, to see who could pick either the most hops or the cleanest hops. He had a large turnout and held a community supper and dance at Turner Hall in downtown St. Helena to announce the winners of the contest. In a speech at the event, Dowdell said that this was a great "illustration of the triumph of white labor over Chinese." He thought that it was a much more practical approach than just repeating "the Chinese must go" over and over, as was frequently done throughout town. He estimated that he paid his white laborers $1,000 to pick the hops in the season, which was kept in St. Helena, "which would otherwise have found its way to China." He also felt that if he could continue this practice, he could "bring in a good class of immigrants" who would settle in town with their families.[63] Despite his optimistic claims, Dowdell was still using Chinese laborers in his hop fields just two years later in 1894. His alternate labor plans, although they garnered publicity, were not sustainable.

The *Napa Journal* reprinted a story from the *Oakland Tribune* accusing Chinese hop pickers elsewhere in California of "mixing a large quantity of small pebbles and clods of dirt with the hops he picks." This would obviously make the bags of harvested hops weigh more, which would result in more pay if the hop pickers were being paid by weight.[64] This was a typical tactic of the local newspapers. They would reprint anti-Chinese stories from around the state in their papers. In this way, they would not be specifically accusing local Chinese laborers of anything wrong, but it would constitute a warning of what could happen locally and leave a negative impression with their readers about the entire local Chinese community.

QUICKSILVER MINING

While the wine business was the fastest-growing industry in late nineteenth-century Napa Valley, it was by no means the only large industry in the area. There was gold, silver, iron and coal in the mountains around the Napa Valley. Unfortunately for aspiring businessmen, the concentrations of minerals or ores was not large enough in most cases to build a successful mining business. There was one exception that managed to be moderately profitable in the late 1800s: quicksilver mines.[65] Quicksilver, or liquid mercury, was used in thermometers and many drugs and chemicals popular in the late nineteenth century. From 1848 until 1882, all quicksilver mining in the United States came from California. Miners would dig up cinnabar ore and melt it to collect the liquid mercury, which would evaporate and then condense in a furnace. The mercury would be collected and transferred to seventy-five-pound iron flasks that would be shipped to various factories. Most quicksilver mines were relatively small, but supply still frequently outpaced demand, so quicksilver never fetched a particularly high price. The high point of domestic production was in 1877, when quicksilver fetched $37.30 per flask and mines generated almost seventy-five thousand flasks. By 1890, it was up to $52.50 per flask, but many mines were either exhausted or had a hard time turning a profit at even that price, and domestic production had slipped to twenty-two thousand flasks.[66] Around 1880, there were at least fifteen quicksilver mines operating in and around the Napa Valley.[67] The price of quicksilver and the number of flasks produced by local quicksilver mines were published in the local newspaper and tracked closely by the public.[68]

Quicksilver mining was hard and dangerous work due to the risks of digging tunnels into the mountainside, as well as the toxicity of the resulting mercury that was extracted from the mined cinnabar ore. Due to the slim profit margins, many mine owners looked for sources of cheap labor to make their mines as successful as possible. The economics of Chinese labor was too attractive for some owners to ignore. Some mines would only hire

Local cinnabar ore with native mercury (quicksilver). The ore would be crushed and heated to release mercury, which could be toxic to miners. *Napa Valley Museum.*

white miners, while other mines would have a mix of Chinese and white miners to keep labor costs low. One example of a mixed mining crew was the Napa Consolidated Quicksilver Mine, also known as the Oat Hill Mine. It generated about 450 flasks per month in 1880 and employed 150 Chinese miners and 115 white miners.[69] By 1898, it still had about 150 Chinese miners on staff, alongside 150 white miners. It was considered at that time one of the largest quicksilver mines in the world.[70] Three of the top four mines in the Napa Valley, which together accounted for more than 80 percent of the flasks produced in 1879, relied heavily on Chinese labor.[71]

The Sulphur Bank Mining Company relied on its Chinese miners so much that it was reluctant to release them even after the 1879 California Constitution declared that Chinese laborers could not be employed by a California corporation. The *Napa Register* did not approve of keeping the Chinese miners on staff and stated, "The Sulphur Bank Mining Company, who have taken very little interest in the new Constitution and the Workingman's agitation, have concluded to go about as they please, at present at least, and continue at the mine with the aid of the Chinese, as heretofore."[72] By February 1880, the Sulphur Mine had succumbed to legal and public pressure. The president of the company, Tiburcio Parrott, had refused to fire the miners and was arrested. He had vowed to fight the clause in the new California Constitution, but the superintendent at the mine told him that the public had become "so bitter against the company for its refusing to discharge its Chinese that it would be best to let them go, and they were accordingly discharged."[73] The following week, the mine was advertising for white miners and offering between $1.75 and $3.00 per day, considerably more than it was paying Chinese miners.[74]

Even though they were hiring replacement laborers, Parrott and the Sulphur Bank Mining Company pursued the claim in U.S. Circuit Court that they should have the right to employ Chinese miners. The court heard the case and, on March 22, 1880, rendered a verdict in favor of Sulphur Bank, declaring that the clause in the California Constitution was illegal because it contravened both the Fourteenth Amendment to the U.S. Constitution and federal treaties with China. The opinion, read by Justice Hoffman, included the following:

> It is an attempt at an unconstitutional object, to drive the Chinese from the country by preventing them from obtaining a living. Corporations have the constitutional right to protect property by employing such labor as they please, subject only to such police regulations as may exist. The law is, as its title shows, directed against the Chinese. The purpose of the law is apparent, and in direct violation of the treaty.[75]

The verdict was greeted with great enthusiasm in the Sulphur Bank Mine and elsewhere. At the Great Western Mine, the "Chinese were, of course, very much elated over the decision, in consequence of which the mine to-day presents the appearance of a Chinese gala day, over which the whites are manifesting considerable enthusiasm."[76] Declaring that a portion of a state constitution was illegal and thus null and void was a significant legal precedent, and it was all due to the efforts of Napa Valley quicksilver mines to keep Chinese miners employed and on the job.

Some mines would not hire Chinese miners no matter the potential labor cost savings. The Reddington Quicksilver Mine, located in the northeast corner of Napa County, was founded in 1860, which made it one of the oldest mines in the area. It formed the center of a company town named Knoxville, which no longer exists, that had about five hundred residents. In 1880, the price of quicksilver was low, and it had reduced its mining crew to about fifty miners. It proudly stated that those fifty are "all white men, there never having been a Chinaman employed about the premises by the present superintendent. The policy of the company is, at present, to employ barely enough men to pay the expense of keeping up the mine, without exhausting the ore bodies at so trifling a profit."[77] The Reddington mine would not even consider having Chinese miners despite significant economic pressures that presumably could have resulted in the closure of the mine entirely.

On the other side of that economic calculus was the Great Western Mine. Based on the hillside of Mount St. Helena, its mining crew were all Chinese. It employed between 200 and 250 Chinese miners continuously from the mid-1870s through the early 1900s. The miners lived and worked at the mine. Their living environment was split into two camps, Camp No. 1 and Brown China Camp, separated based on which region in China from which the men emigrated.[78] Miners who lived at Camp No. 1 were from the Canton area. Most of the miners spoke little or no English and worked the backbreaking, dangerous mining jobs. There were some Chinese miners who spoke English and would manage the other miners' business affairs, hold the more important jobs at the mine site or work in the superintendent's house.[79] The wage discrepancy between Chinese and white laborers was considerable. The average wage for a Chinese miner in the 1890s was $1.25 per day versus $2.25 per day for a white miner. Senior mechanics (all white) could make as much as $4.00 per day.[80]

Another benefit of having a predominately Chinese labor force was the ability to rapidly shrink or grow in size depending on the market rate for quicksilver and whether the mine was producing well by working closely with Chinese labor bosses. The *St. Helena Star* reported in 1886 that "[s]everal Chinese have been discharged from the Gt. Western Quicksilver Mine, and it has been reported that seventy-five in all will be sent away. This wholesale discharge of Mongols is made necessary by the small amount of cinnabar at present found at the mine."[81] Presumably they were recalled when the mine started producing again. Unlike at the Sulphur Bank Mine, when the 1879 California Constitution was passed the Great Western temporarily closed the mines and did not even try to hire white replacement workers. It claimed that "they cannot employ white labor and pay expenses."[82] The entire economic model of the Great Western Mine, the second-largest mine in the area, was predicated on using Chinese miners.

The camps where the Chinese miners at the Great Western lived were a jumble of hastily constructed shacks built by the miners themselves out of whatever materials they could get their hands on. They lacked basic sanitation. There was no central eating hall, so each man cooked his own meal of rice with a small fire in front of his house. The miners wore "a dungaree costume similar to the work clothes of sailors" and their distinctive large straw hat.[83]

China Camp at the Great Western Mine, where Chinese miners lived in the late 1890s. *From Helen Goss's* The Life and Death of a Quicksilver Mine.

The camps followed the same labor-boss model that was used in the vineyards and during railroad construction. Each camp had a boss, who would work with the mine superintendent to determine how much each miner was owed and then would be responsible for distributing the wages to the miners directly. Helen Goss, who grew up in the camp as a young daughter of the mine superintendent, tells of the labor boss of Brown China Camp named Ah Shee. He was well educated, larger than most of the other miners, an excellent worker and was trusted by the superintendent and his family. He made $1.50 per day and was the highest-paid miner. He had his employer keep a savings account for him in San Francisco, and by the time Ah Shee was ready to return to China, he had accumulated nearly $6,000. The labor boss of Camp No. 1 was Ah Key, who was smaller than Ah Shee but was adept at keeping the peace among the men in the camps, which was a constant concern.

Violence occurred somewhat frequently within the camp. The most serious violent outbreak occurred in 1880. Andrew Rocca, the mine superintendent, wrote to his fiancée about a "bloody row" among the Chinese miners that involved both camps and about 125 men. Rocca said that 4 or 5 were "badly cut." The riot was quelled when he arrived in the middle of the camps with his rifle, which he never fired. He did say that had he "not been here there would have been thirty or forty of them killed."[84]

In addition to sometimes violent quarrels within the camps, the work itself was quite dangerous. The mines were constructed by blasting and digging deep underground by workers with minimal safety equipment. The tunnels were supported by large timbers that could fall and crush unsuspecting miners. There were multiple furnaces cooking the cinnabar ore all the time to generate the quicksilver, causing the air in the mine shafts to become increasingly hot and likely toxic. The Chinese laborers served as miners, furnace men and, the most dangerous job, a "sootman." The sootmen had to crawl into the hot furnace condensers and clean out the baked-on mercury. They would eventually succumb to mercury poisoning after long-term exposure to mercury vapors and turn into "shaking, toothless wrecks." One sootman at the mine was named Ah Cat. He was known to the superintendent's family because he liked coffee and would frequently go to the superintendent's house for a cup. The family noticed that eventually, "poor old Cat put his face to the cup on the back steps and then hardly be able to hold still enough to drink."[85] Ah Cat likely was suffering from mercury poisoning, including lack of muscle coordination and muscle weakness.[86]

There was also the constant threat of fires, from either the furnaces, forest fires or from fires within the camps themselves. The *Weekly Calistogian* reported in 1898 that two Chinese miners were killed outright and twenty more were wounded in an explosion in China Camp No. 2 at the Napa Consolidated Quicksilver Mine. Some Chinese miners were reportedly setting off firecrackers in their cabin early in the morning before their

The miners (all Chinese) and management/support staff (all white) at the Great Western Mine in 1879. *From Helen Goss's* The Life and Death of a Quicksilver Mine.

shift began. The firecrackers set the cabin on fire, and the fire spread to an adjacent cabin, where a large quantity of gunpowder and blasting caps were stored under the floorboards. The miners were not supposed to keep explosives in their cabins, but it could have been stored in anticipation of the upcoming Chinese New Year. Once the gunpowder got hot enough, the "house which concealed the powder was blown to smithereens, nothing whatever remaining on its site. Two of the Chinamen were instantly killed." Five buildings were destroyed.[87]

GENERAL CONSTRUCTION AND FARMING

Much of the early physical infrastructure work in the Napa Valley was performed by Chinese laborers. In both the 1870 and the 1880 censuses, the "laborer" job classification was the largest category for Chinese residents. As early as 1873, the *Napa Reporter* said that "twenty-seven Chinamen and three white men" were building the first road between Calistoga and a quicksilver mine in nearby Pope Valley.[88] In 1875, a local vintner named John Lewelling hired Chinese to build fences around his vineyard.[89] In 1877, Simpson Thompson cut the wages of white laborers who were building a road in Napa, and they promptly struck and left the worksite. Thompson was able to quickly replace them with Chinese laborers, who were willing to work for the lesser wage. This economic tactic was successful as, within a year, the white laborers returned to the construction project at the lower wage.[90] Stories like this made white employers happy but undoubtedly contributed to the resentment of Chinese workers by white workers who were either displaced or threatened with displacement.

Chinese laborers also worked on winery construction projects, which could be dangerous for workers. In 1877, Chinese laborers were digging a wine cellar for C. Lemme near St. Helena when a worker was killed due to a partial cave-in.[91] It could also be risky for the winery owners who hired Chinese laborers. Terrill Grigsby hired many Chinese laborers to help construct his winery in 1878. He also used Chinese workers around his farm to harvest wheat, cut hay and so on. His barn was destroyed by fire, and he lost four hundred sacks of barley and fifty tons of hay, among other items. He had been threatened by letter during the winery construction that if he did not stop using Chinese labor, he would be "burned out." He believed that the fire was in retribution for his reliance on Chinese workers.[92]

One of the earliest examples of winery construction was described by a reporter in 1863 of Chinese doing "inside work" at Buena Vista winery in neighboring Sonoma Valley: "On the same floor we found four Chinamen filling, corking, wiring, etc. Champagne bottles....There are now in progress three cellars, close to the press house. These are all being blasted and excavated by Chinese. They are to be twenty-six feet wide, thirteen feet in height, and three hundred feet long."[93] The Chinese were doing work, some quite perilous, that no one else was willing to do. As an article in *Overland Monthly* magazine said in 1869, "Well, if white labor is as difficult to be obtained as is reported, and as indeed it must be, since wages are so high, what would these farmers do but for the Chinamen?"[94]

Chinese laborers were also hired out on an individual basis to work on farms. One of the few accounts of how locals interacted with Chinese laborers comes from an oral history of John York. York was an early California pioneer who moved from Tennessee to the Napa Valley in 1845 at age twenty-five and lived in St. Helena from 1850 until his death in 1910. By some accounts, he had the first commercial vineyard in the Napa Valley. In the late 1880s, he employed a Chinese laborer to help chop wood on his farm. When the task was complete, York and the Chinese hired hand disagreed on the number of cords of wood that had been chopped. The Chinese man called York a liar, and for that offense, York "grabbed a two-foot stick of wood about 5-inches through, and just as the Chinaman turned to avoid the blow, he hit him on the back of the head." Amazingly, the hired hand was able to stagger to his feet and escape with his life—presumably without getting paid.[95] Clearly a white farmer had no fear of being charged with attempted murder of a Chinese man who was not a citizen and almost certainly would get no justice from local law enforcement.

THE RAILROAD

In the second half of the 1800s, railroads were big business across the nation and California, as well as within the Napa Valley. The Central Pacific Railroad and the Union Pacific Railroad companies were chosen to build the First Transcontinental Railroad in the United States in 1862. The Central Pacific was faced with a huge labor shortage during construction. It recruited twelve thousand laborers from China and Hong Kong to build the 690-mile railway through the Sierra Nevada Mountains and across Nevada into Utah. The railroad was completed in 1869 with the joining of the eastbound and westbound tracks at Promontory Point, Utah.[96] The work of the Chinese on railroads continued for years after that. Chinese workers helped to build and maintain seventy-one other rail lines and train depots throughout the United States, including several in the Napa Valley.[97]

Several hundred Chinese workers were brought in from San Francisco to build the original set of tracks for the Napa Valley Railroad in 1867. The route went for twenty-six miles from Napa to Calistoga. Construction was rapid as the valley floor was generally level. It began in downtown Napa in March 1867 and had reached Oakville by September and St. Helena by February 1868. It reached its final destination in Calistoga in August 1868, just sixteen months after construction began. Many of the Chinese railroad workers on that project stayed in the Napa Valley and found other employment.[98]

By 1880, ninety-eight Chinese laborers were living in Napa and employed by the Central Pacific Railroad, which by that time owned the Napa Valley Railroad. This made the railroad company the single biggest employer of Chinese labor in the city of Napa and the third-largest source of employment in the entire Napa Valley. The Chinese rail workers lived in two large communal living centers on the east end of town near the railroad tracks. One building had fifty-six residents, and one had forty-two residents. Unsurprisingly, due to the recruitment efforts by the Central Pacific, all the Chinese railroad employees were listed in the census as being from Hong Kong, while almost every other Chinese resident of the Napa Valley was said to be from Canton, or, more broadly, "China."[99]

They worked a variety of difficult jobs for the railroads. In 1883, the *Napa Register* reported that a work crew of 60 or more men, including Chinese laborers, was grading and leveling the land for the Napa and Lake Railroad. The crew had completed seven miles of the project through mountainous terrain.[100] In early September 1886, 215 Chinese laborers were working on grading and constructing thirty miles of railroad track for the Rutherford and Clear Lake Railroad, which was scheduled to be operational the following year.[101] Three weeks later, 40 additional Chinese laborers were sent up from San Francisco on the Napa Valley Railroad to assist on the Rutherford Railroad construction.[102] The Napa and Lake Railroads and the Rutherford and Clear Lake Railroads were smaller, narrow-gauge railroads that branched off the main line. The work could be very dangerous. The *St. Helena Star* reported on a gas explosion during the digging of a tunnel for the South Pacific Coast Railroad that killed 30 Chinese railroad laborers and injured others. No white workers were killed and only two were injured.[103]

From the very beginning of railroads in the Napa Valley, the Chinese were instrumental in their construction and maintenance. The railroads

Railroad trestle bridge in Napa circa 1905. Building railroad bridges like this one would have been typical work for Chinese railroad laborers. *Courtesy of the Napa County Historical Society, ID 2014.25.1.*

allowed for the easier movement of people and goods up and down the valley and gave farmers, including vineyard owners, a reliable way to export their products. Vineyards were planted all along the railroad lines and are still there today. The assessed value of land in the Napa County increased dramatically after the arrival of the railroad. In 1864, the assessed property value of all lands in the county was $1.6 million. By 1880, that value had increased to $9.1 million, more than a fivefold increase. As an editorial in the *Napa Register* put it:

> *A person would be an idiot should he deny that much of the increase of property in Napa Valley is due to the presence of the railroad. The railroad has stimulated the planting of vines, the building of costly and magnificent wine cellars, the growth of all the towns along its borders, and the increase of all the industries in the valley of Napa and contributed millions to the assessable value of the property of the county.*[104]

The Napa Valley of 1880 would not have been successful without the railroads; the railroads would not have been there in 1880 without the labor of hundreds of Chinese workers.

Chapter 3

URBAN NAPA VALLEY

In the more urban parts of the Valley, Chinese laborers worked in the tannery industry and as domestic servants, cooks, shopkeepers, laundry owners and vegetable peddlers (also known as truck gardeners). Living and working in urban areas provided a different set of challenges for the Chinese workers compared to those working in a more rural, outdoor setting. Yet the same economic drivers that made the Chinese labor contribution critical and successful in the countryside continued to be true in the cities as well. Chinese workers had no choice but to do jobs that many white townspeople did not want to do, or they did similar jobs for lower wages. For many businesses, employing Chinese labor was the only way to survive or be profitable enough to expand. In other areas, like domestic service, inexpensive Chinese labor provided an element of luxury and privilege to townspeople that they would not have had otherwise.

CHINESE STORES

Chinese stores in various Napa Valley Chinatowns served as central hubs for many Chinese workers and provided a sense of the culture they left behind. Many Chinese merchants not only sold goods and foods from China, but they also served as banks, post offices, hostels and employment offices. Workers from around the area would converge on the stores during holidays or when they needed a place to stay. The function of the store

Chinese man posing for a portrait in St. Helena. *Courtesy of the St. Helena Historical Society.*

as a post office was critically important for seasonal workers to have a place to receive their mail and provide a means to send mail back to their home villages. The stores would serve as a surrogate bank or pawn shop where workers could keep their personal valuables, weapons and money for safekeeping. In larger Chinatowns, every district from which Chinese workers emigrated would have its own store.[105]

The occupation of shop owner had several benefits compared to being a laborer from China within U.S. immigration policy. Merchants were allowed to travel back and forth to China and bring their wives and families with them. Chan Wah Jack, a Napa Chinatown merchant, was able to take advantage of this distinction when he returned to Napa with his wife and family from China in 1898. Chinese claiming to be merchants had to provide papers to the Immigration Service declaring the amount of money and value of the stock they had in their businesses to qualify.

As early as 1875, Chinese merchants were providing services to local Chinese workers in the Napa Valley. Many of these stores ran advertisements in local papers, providing us with one of the few glimpses of Chinese directly speaking to the larger community. Wah Chung said that he had three hundred laborers ready to work the fields. He printed out papers "American style, which advertise him to furnish help of every kind."[106]

He had competition from Quong Goon Loong, who in 1876 opened his own store in St. Helena. His store contained a variety of goods from China to sell both to local Chinese and curious white townspeople. He also could furnish labor to vineyard owners and farmers who needed it. His location near Sulphur Spring Creek meant that it was in the heart of St. Helena's Chinatown.

"Ginger" owned and ran Ginger's China Store for more than twenty-five years, on and off, in St. Helena and was a constant fixture in Chinatown. In 1877, he was called by the *St. Helena Star* "the leading Chinese businessman" in St. Helena.[107] Unfortunately, his business failed a year later with debts of $1,000.[108] By the end of 1878, he was replaced at his China Store by Fook Lee, who expanded his offerings of Chinese goods and labor to include a boardinghouse and an "intelligence office," which was a term for an employment office where people who needed to hire Chinese laborers

NEW ADVERTISEMENTS.

QUONG GOON LOONG,

STORE NEAR SPRING CREEK, ACROSS THE
BRIDGE, ST . HELENA, CAL.

— DEALER IN —

CHINA GOODS.

China Hats, Slippers, Tea, Sugar, Rice,
Etc.

China labor Furnished. n31

Left: An advertisement for Quong Goon Loong's China Goods Store in the April 22, 1876 edition of the *St. Helena Star.*

Below: Fook Lee's first advertisement after replacing "Ginger" at the China Store in St. Helena. *From* St. Helena Star, *December 13, 1878.*

Fook Lee,
CHINA STORE,
BOARDING HOUSE & INTELLI-
GENCE OFFICE,
MAIN STREET, ACROSS THE R. R. BRIDGE,
St . Helena, Napa County, California. China
Goods sold and China Labor furnished.

for a job would go to get workers.[109] Most intelligence offices in the Napa Valley were run by Chinese shopkeepers, which explains why, in 1883, Napa County passed an ordinance assessing a twenty-dollar annual license fee on every intelligence office.[110] Ironically, Napa's Anti-Chinese League three years later wanted to open its own intelligence office to make it easier for employers to find white workers to hire. It petitioned the county to rescind the original license fee put in place to penalize the Chinese shop owners because now it would have to pay the license fee as well.[111]

Ginger recovered from his bankruptcy by 1880 and co-sponsored the annual Chinese New Year's fireworks display with Quong Goon.[112] A year later, he was solely credited in the *Star* for the fireworks display, which called him "the representative Chinaman of St. Helena" and said that he "always does the honors handsomely on these occasions."[113]

A fire in St. Helena's Chinatown in 1884 provides an indication of the value of the merchandise they carried. The fire, which eventually destroyed half of Chinatown, raced through the poorly constructed wooden buildings, and four stores lost contents valued at $300, $500, $500 and $1,500 (equivalent to approximately $8,000 to $41,000 today). The buildings themselves, owned by a St. Helena real estate developer named John Gillam, were valued at $1,000.[114] Gillam just a week later declared that he was rebuilding the burned stores as soon as possible, and the displaced Chinese merchants were already negotiating the lease price to move back in.

In Napa, the main China Store was operated by Chan Wah Jack. He took over running his brothers' China Store, named Sang Lung, in 1898. The Sang Lung store was destroyed in a 1900 fire that raced through Chinatown, but in 1902, Chan Wah Jack opened a new establishment called Lai Hing that not only was operated as a general store for Chinese food and merchandise but also functioned as a kind of bank for Chinese workers. The workers were trying to save money to send back home to China. When they deposited at the store, Wah Jack's son Shuck Chan remembers, they "would remove the temptation of gambling it all away." In addition to banking services, Lai Hing also functioned as a yok choy po (herb shop) where workers could get

Young Chinese men in Napa's Chinatown in front of the Lai Hing Company Store. *Courtesy of the Napa County Historical Society, 2012.2.99.*

herbal medicines.[115] Suey Ping, one of Chan Wah Jack's daughters, recalled how Lai Hing Company was a favorite not only of Chinese workers but also of townspeople throughout Napa:

> *The Lai Hing store was well patronized by white customers who found among the merchandise offered many attractive articles of Oriental design. Chinese candies and nuts and a specially processed delicacy—dried abalone which some of us mistakenly called China clam—were favored items.*[116]

THE TANNERY

Chinese workers were involved in small-scale manufacturing throughout California. They were significant elements of the workforce in the manufacturing of woolen textiles, clothing, shoes and cigars in San Francisco and beyond.[117] In Napa, the industry with the most significant Chinese labor presence was leather manufacturing in tanneries. In the late nineteenth century, Napa was nearly as famous as a center of leather production as it was for its wine production. Just like in the wine industry, inexpensive and reliable Chinese labor was critical in the formative period of tanneries. Napa leather was used for a variety of products like baseballs, baseball gloves, patent leather shoes and outerwear. The term "Nappa leather," still in use today to indicate ultra-luxurious leather, was derived from the process developed at Sawyer Tannery in Napa and patented in 1875.[118]

The Sawyer Tannery Company was founded by F.A. Sawyer in 1869.[119] The leather manufacturing company started small and was reliant on Chinese workers from the very beginning. In 1870, it employed one white laborer and four Chinese laborers. They could process up to 125 sheepskins per day. By the mid-1870s, the company had increased its workforce to include twelve white laborers and seventy Chinese laborers. By 1880, it had electrified the plant and expanded the buildings and was processing 2,000 sheepskins per day.[120]

The 1880 census reported that there were sixty-three Chinese workers living in a communal living situation on Grant Street in Napa with an occupation of "Tannery." This was the second-largest group of Chinese living together in Napa, just behind Chinatown. They were all men from the Canton region and ranged in age from twenty-two-year-old Hong Sing to forty-seven-year-old Ah Lee.[121] They served as the backbone of the tannery workforce.

The workforce of the Sawyer Tannery, circa 1878, was about 80 percent Chinese laborers. *From* Illustrations of Napa County, California: With Historical Sketch.

Up until 1885, the Sawyer Tannery was the single largest private employer of Chinese workers in Napa Valley, according to the *Napa County Reporter*. This changed in 1886 with the inauguration of the first formal anti-Chinese movement in Napa. The tannery, somewhat surprisingly for a business that owed its early success to Chinese workers, was a participant in that movement, terminating fifty Chinese workers in January 1886 and replacing them with white workers. The *Reporter* extolled its "progress" in this area and said, "They will continue in this good work until their employes [*sic*] are all white people if such a thing is possible."[122] The Sawyer Tannery, which was heavily reliant on its predominantly Chinese workforce at its inception, bowed to anti-Chinese pressure quickly.

Domestic Servants and Cooks

The largest occupation across all Chinese working in the Napa Valley was working within a home as domestic servants and cooks. The number of

Chinese workers engaged in work as domestic servants is one of the few occupations that saw a decrease in census data between 1870 and 1880 (see Table 5 and Table 6 in the appendix) from 56 to 44. But the number of cooks rose from 10 to 151—together those professions formed a significant percentage of Chinese employment. Presumably all "domestic servants" worked within people's homes, but "cooks" described Chinese workers who were either cooks within people's homes as servants or worked as cooks on farms or in hotels.

Chinese servants were highly valued, as they were indispensable for a well-kept home or estate. Many families, if they could afford it, employed a Chinese man as a gardener, servant or cook. A wealthy family could afford a whole staff of Chinese servants. Chinese were trusted to care for their children and keep them safe. The Chinese domestics, in turn, respected their employers. Typically, a Chinese servant would be taught English by the mistress of the household, and he would learn how to prepare American dishes, set a fine table and understand how to maintain the household. There was mutual respect and trust between the servant and the family.

Almost all of these domestic servants and cooks were men, and they were frequently referred to as "China Boys." Robert Louis Stevenson wrote about seeking out a Chinese domestic servant to help him and his family as they spent the summer in Calistoga:

> We had found what an amount of labour it cost to support life in our red canyon; and it was the dearest desire of our hearts to get a China-boy to go along with us when we returned.[123]

Traditionally, young unmarried white women would serve as servants in a household, but it could be problematic to find and keep a good servant:

> The Chinese servant, as a rule, was more willing to do what was required of him than a white woman who was likely to offer objections at every turn, insisting on superior accommodations and inconvenient privileges. He was no more a natural cook than he was a natural gold digger. But he was always willing to work in any station, and he accommodated himself to the service of the kitchen and dining room.[124]

Chinese servants, despite language and cultural barriers, provided a good substitute. Jue Joe, discussed earlier in this book, even worked as a domestic servant in his fifties to help earn money to rebuild his farming fortune.

One Chinese domestic servant in the Napa Valley was Ah Hing. Hing served as the cook and kind of a general manager of the Lyman household for more than thirty years, from 1884 to 1919. The Lyman house, situated on a small farm in St. Helena, consisted of a family of four, including two sons. According to recollections set down in 1964 by the younger son W.W. Lyman, Hing had a diverse set of responsibilities, including cooking family meals, ensuring that the boys got up on time for school and did their homework, feeding the various animals around the farms and supervising other Chinese workers who were occasionally employed to work in the garden. He was trained how to cook by Lyman's mother, who liked food prepared in the "southern style." Everything had lots of cream added, but since the farm had twenty-five cattle, that was never an issue.

Lyman said that Hing took his job very seriously and "tried to exert his control in every direction," and he was "an invaluable servant to us." Hing went back to China occasionally, as many Chinese workers in the Napa Valley did. He was replaced during his absences by other Chinese cooks who would temporarily fill Hing's role. In 1919, Hing returned to China

Ah Hing was the cook and general manager for the Lyman family for thirty-five years. *Courtesy of the family of Li Li Lyman.*

Ah Hing with the Lyman family at dinner under the large fig tree next to the Lyman house, 1906. *Courtesy of the family of Li Li Lyman.*

permanently when his failing eyesight made his work at the Lyman house increasingly difficult.[125]

In Hing's case, he was a domestic servant on a small family farm in St. Helena, where he may have felt fairly isolated. Chinese servants in downtown Napa lived near one another, and that would have provided a very different sense of community. Several families on Third Street in downtown Napa, which still has many of the charming Victorian houses on tree-lined streets that were present back in 1880, employed Chinese servants.

Richard Wylie, who in 1880 was a thirty-nine-year-old minister, originally from Ohio, lived with his wife, Harriett, thirty-seven. In their house was Hatie Smith, age eighteen, and their Chinese servant, Ah Sing, age twenty. Even though they did not have young children at home, his job as a minister required entertaining families from his congregation frequently, and he presumably made frequent use of Ah Sing's services. Richard also preached at the Chinese Chapel in downtown Napa, so he was very comfortable with Chinese people of all occupations.

Two doors down lived James Thompson, age forty-six, who had a farm on the outskirts of town and lived with his thirty-four-year-old wife, Mary. They were both from Pennsylvania. They had three children: fifteen-year-old George, twelve-year-old Margaret and six-year-old William. They also had a Chinese cook, a fifteen-year-old named Ah Chung.

Seven doors down from them lived the Spensers. Dennis Spenser was a thirty-five-year-old attorney, originally from Missouri, who lived with his wife, Helen, twenty-seven, and their two young children, four-year-old Lloyd and two-year-old Ruthie. As an attorney, he was financially well off and could afford a live-in servant. They employed Ah Chang, a nineteen-year-old, to help them out around the house. Four doors down from the Spensers was a boardinghouse or apartment where four Chinese men lived, all of whom worked in a laundry in town. The laundry was managed by twenty-one-year-old Ah Que, and he had three employees who also lived there: nineteen-year-old Ah Ching Soy, twenty-nine-year-old Ching Toon and thirty-six-year-old Quang Moon. This area of Napa had a significant population of Chinese workers interspersed with the white population.

CHINESE LAUNDRIES

Chinese workers were employed in many different occupations in Napa Valley towns, but no occupation matched the controversy and vitriol surrounding the laundry industry. According to the U.S. Census figures, about forty-three Chinese worked in the laundry business in 1870, and fifty-five Chinese worked in that business in 1880. It was the fourth-most popular occupation for Chinese in 1870 and had dropped to fifth-most popular in 1880. The Chinese had a monopoly on this business, which caused great consternation among some white townspeople and business leaders.[126]

Throughout the 1870s, the Chinese wash house owners were allowed to perform their laundry services in Napa, St. Helena and Calistoga with relatively little controversy. The earliest mention of Chinese laundries in the local papers was in a news article in the *St. Helena Star* on August 18, 1876, which, though brief, foreshadowed troubles to come: "In this small pox [*sic*] season citizens will do well to avoid Chinese laundries, that race being the proverbial habitat of the dreadful scourge. Patronize white institutions." This simple article managed to both denigrate the hygiene of Chinese workers and accuse them of spreading a deadly disease. It was also a call to arms of sorts to patronize white-owned businesses over Chinese-owned businesses.

While white-owned laundries were occasionally started, it was inevitable that one of their main value propositions was that they were run by non-Chinese owners. There also was a pervasive cultural idea that white women, not Chinese men, could or should be running laundry businesses because it was in their domestic sphere. In

French Laundry.

WASHING AND IRONING neatly done on the most reasonable terms. Give your laundrying to a deserving white woman in preference to Chinese, MRS. KRAMER, deodtf. Cor. of Coombs and Clay Streets.

Laundry advertisement from June 14, 1880 *Napa Valley Register*, with an explicit racial call to action.

1882, the *Napa County Reporter* ran an article about the incorporation of the Women's Protective League, whose purpose was to encourage the "introduction of women in various branches of domestic industry."[127] This aligns with an ad placed in the *Napa Valley Register* two years earlier for a laundry that explicitly contrasted a white woman–owned business with a Chinese-owned one—"give your laundering to a deserving white woman in preference to Chinese."[128]

In 1883, Napa County passed an ordinance that specifically targeted the Chinese-male dominated industry and did not affect any woman-owned laundries. According to the ordinance, "Every male person carrying on the laundry business, and every proprietor of a laundry where male persons are employed shall obtain a license from the license tax collector and pay therefore three dollars ($3.00) per quarter."[129] Assuming that the Chinese had a monopoly or near-monopoly on the laundry business in the county, a twelve-dollar annual tax assessed on each Chinese man working in the laundry had just one purpose: make it harder for Chinese owners to stay in the laundry business. It seems that the Chinese owners were able to absorb the tax and still maintain their competitive price advantage such that they retained their monopoly status.

In the mid-1880s, the anti-Chinese laundry forces, spearheaded by local newspapers, took a new tack. They put forth a concerted effort in multiple towns in the Napa Valley to solicit and encourage white-owned laundry facilities. The *Napa Register* and the *St. Helena Star* both called for "white laundries" in their cities. The *Star* put out an editorial in early 1885 that read, "St. Helena cries out for the clear-headed, enterprising individual who will establish a white laundry within her boundaries."[130] The *Star* happily reported a few months later to its readers about the upcoming opening of a white-owned laundry that would "rescue them from the thralldom of the filthy Chinese laundries." The new owner, Mr. Henry Lange, had "already engaged a number of competent white laundrymen, and will, under no circumstances, employ Chinese." The readers were assured that the prices "will not amount to much more than present Chinese rates."[131]

In late 1885, the *Register* editorialized that "The Chinese wash-house must go. Public sentiment and the establishment of white laundries in towns the size of Napa say so."[132] In early 1886, the *Register* bemoaned the fact that the Calistoga White Laundry had to shut down, not because of "want of patronage" but "because the amount that people in general are willing to pay for their washing will not compensate white laborers for their services." It was a shame, it declared, because a successful, white-run laundry would have finally rid the town of "one or two Chinese wash-houses and their objectionable tenants."[133]

The conclusion of the *Register* was that white laborers could not compete economically with laundries that used Chinese laborers unless they had a technological advantage. In February 1886, the paper announced that three businessmen were considering opening up a "first class steam laundry in our town. When it is once in running order they will be able to compete in prices and excel in quality of work any Mongolian wash-house in our city."[134] Apparently, this was not a moment too soon because one month later, the paper had to announce that a traditional non-steam white-owned laundry in Napa had to close because the furnace was damaged and "with hand labor we could not begin to compete with the Chinese." Ironically, in that same issue where it reported on the closing of the white-owned laundry, that same laundry was running an ad touting how it could do the wash "without the aid of the Chinese."[135]

Sam Kee was a successful Chinese laundry owner who established his business in Napa in 1879. In 1881, he was advertising in the local newspaper to drum up business. By 1885, he was setting off fifty dollars' worth of firecrackers in front of his shop to celebrate the Chinese New

Could Hold Out No Longer

The Napa White Laundry, opposite the REGISTER office, suspended operations last Tuesday. It was the intention of Mr. Palmer, its proprietor, to keep the institution running until a steam laundry was started here, but an accident to the furnace this morning made it advisable to terminate the business at once. "With hand labor we could not begin to compete with the Chinese," said Mr. Palmer Tuesday, "though I hope the white laundry about to be started on McKenstry street, and the steam laundry talked of may find it profitable."

An 1886 article declaring the closure of that laundry service because "they could not begin to compete with the Chinese." *From the* Napa Register, *March 5, 1886.*

Year, much to the delight of several hundred spectators.[136] Sam Kee was establishing himself as a respected businessman in Napa.

However, the City of Napa, as did many cities in California, continued to pass ordinances to push Chinese laundries out of business. By 1887, the city had enacted Napa City Ordinance No. 146, which contained the following key sections:

Section 1. It shall be unlawful for any person or persons to establish, maintain, or carry on the business of a public laundry or wash-house, where articles are cleansed for hire, within the following prescribed limits in the city of Napa: Commencing at the south-easterly corner…

Section 2. Any public laundry or wash-house, established, maintained, or carried on in violation of this ordinance, is hereby declared to be a nuisance.

Section 8. Any person violating any provision of this ordinance shall, upon conviction thereof, before any court having jurisdiction to try the offense, be punished by a fine not exceeding one hundred dollars, and an alternate judgment may be given requiring such person to be imprisoned until said fine is paid, not to exceed one day for each dollar of the fine.

The ordinance was put in place to specifically target Chinese laundries, as it had a geographic limit that included Chinatown and various Chinese businesses in town. On April 8, 1887, a warrant was issued for the arrest of Sam Kee and two others for violating the laundry ordinance. He was charged with a "misdemeanor by maintaining and carrying on a public laundry, where articles are washed and cleansed for hire, at a house situated on Main street, between First and Pearl streets in the city of Napa, contrary to ordinance 146 of said city of Napa; prohibiting the establishment, carrying on, or maintaining of public laundries or wash-houses in certain limits."[137] By April 21, 1887, the case had been heard, and Sam Kee was convicted of violating the laundry ordinance and sent to jail.[138] He vowed to appeal, and the very next day, he posted $100 bail and appealed his case to the U.S. District Court in San Francisco, challenging the legality of the ordinance. The court agreed to hear the case on May 2, and District Judge Sawyer overturned the Napa guilty verdict in favor of Sam Kee. Sawyer wrote:

The laundry business has been carried on by the petitioner and his predecessors, at the location occupied by him, for 20 years, and by the petitioner himself 8 years. There is nothing tending in the slightest degree to show that this laundry is, in fact, a nuisance, and the uncontradicted allegations of the petition are that it is not. So far as appears, it is only made a nuisance by the arbitrary declaration of the ordinance; and it is beyond the power of the common council, by its simple fiat to make that a nuisance which is not so in fact. Yates v. Milwaukee, 10 Wall. 505. To make an occupation, indispensable to the health and comfort of civilized man, and the use of the property necessary to carry it out, a nuisance, by a more arbitrary declaration in a city ordinance, and suppress it as such, is simply to confiscate the property, and deprive its owner of it without due process of law. It also abridges the liberty of the owner to select his own occupation and his own methods in the pursuit of happiness, and thereby prevents him from enjoying his rights, privileges, and immunities, and deprives him of equal protection of the laws secured to every person by the constitution of the United States.

On the authority of the cases cited, without repeating the arguments so elaborately presented therein, the ordinance is held to be void, as being in contravention of the constitution of the United States. The prisoner is entitled to be discharged. Let him be discharged.[139]

This was a significant victory against local anti-Chinese discrimination ordinances, and this case was cited more than twenty times over the next two decades across the country from California to Oklahoma in cases challenging local ordinances.[140] How did a local Napa laundry owner pay a $100 bail and challenge the case so quickly? He was represented in court by San Francisco attorney Thomas Riordan, who had represented Chinese litigants in San Francisco before. The case was supported financially by the Chinese Six Companies to establish the precedent for other Chinese laundries in the Bay Area and beyond.[141]

The City of Napa was not done with Sam Kee. Perhaps in retribution for the nullification of City Ordinance No. 146, the city arrested Sam Kee again, as well as six of his employees, on June 15, 1887, for violating City Ordinance No. 158, which forbade work in a public laundry on Sundays. Again, Sam Kee vowed to challenge the ordinance.[142] This time, Sam Kee had allies in unexpected places. Reverend Richard Wylie of the First Presbyterian Church in Napa and a sponsor of the Chinese Chapel, a church in downtown Napa dedicated to Christianizing its Chinese residents, argued in a sermon the following week that the arrest of Sam Kee and his employees for working on a Sunday in a laundry was arbitrary. Wylie sermonized, "Houses of ill-fame may blot and blight by their presence and be undisturbed. There may be assaults upon life and no searching investigation as to their cause. But the Chinaman who works on Sunday must be made an example of."[143] Regardless of the help from the pulpit, on July 6, Sam Kee and his partner Ah Hay were fined eleven dollars each for working on a Sunday and ended up not appealing the verdict.[144]

By the end of the 1800s, Sam Kee had become somewhat famous. He was featured in a 1901 history book about Napa, with the following article describing his business dealings, although it did not mention his legal challenges:

LAUNDRY OF SAM KEE

He was born in China; came to Napa about twenty years ago, and has been in the laundry business ever since. His laundry is situated on N. Main street, No 58, next to Kyser's furniture store.

Sam Kee has the oldest established laundry in Napa county, and ever has given the greatest satisfaction to his patrons. Sam Kee is married, having a wife and one child in China.

He gives employment to six other Chinamen in his laundry. The time is now rapidly approaching when Sam Kee will be able to sell out his business

Photograph of Sam Kee's building taken in 1968. Sam Kee moved his laundry business to this building in the 1920s. *Courtesy of the Napa County Historical Society, 1973.6.35.*

and return to China with enough American dollars to enable him to live the
life of a nobleman in his own land and at last lay his bones down in the
sacred soil of the Celestial Kingdom.[145]

Sam is the only Chinese person mentioned by name in a book that is almost five hundred pages long. The article was in error in that Sam was not on the verge of moving back to China to live the life of a nobleman. Sam Kee was still in the laundry business in 1907 when he moved from his laundry on Main Street down the road a few blocks to the "Brown building on N. Main street, formerly occupied by Cook & Rojas' paint shop."[146] A laundry business under the name "Sam Kee Laundry" operated in downtown Napa until the 1970s.

TRUCK GARDENERS

Chinese truck gardeners, or vegetable peddlers, were an important part of the agricultural food chain throughout California in the late 1800s. They typically grew their vegetables on their own plots of land and then brought their produce to cities and towns, where it was sold on carts or other modes of transportation. This occupation started in the mining counties of California to help feed miners, but by the 1870s, it had spread throughout California, including Napa County. They combined production with merchandising, and they were California's earliest retail distributors of fresh produce.[147] The 1880 census documents three Chinese farmers in the Napa Valley: Ah Jim and Ah Yen in Napa and How Fung & Company in St. Helena. Ah Jim had eighteen acres under cultivation, Ah Yen had four acres and How Fung had six acres. Each estimated the value of their products produced that year at around $1,000.[148]

The City of Napa strongly discouraged Chinese vegetable peddlers. In 1880, it passed City Ordinance No. 50 for Fixing and Regulating Peddler's License Tax. It said, in part:

> *Sec. 2. Every person engaged in the itinerate vending, hawking, or peddling*
> *of fruits, vegetables or other agricultural productions; soda, beer, ale, wines*
> *or liquors, shall pay for a license tax to do the same, the sum of twenty*
> *dollars per month, provided, that no license shall be required for the vending*
> *of fruits, vegetables, or other agricultural productions which shall have been*
> *grown or produced by the parties vending the same.*[149]

There may have been three Chinese farmers in 1880, but there were likely many more vegetable peddlers who did not own their farms but looked to make a living by selling other farmers' produce throughout town. A twenty-dollar monthly license tax would have certainly dissuaded many Chinese peddlers. St. Helena had a similar ordinance, and the town finance committee denied the renewal of a vegetable peddler license to a Chinese man because he failed to produce an affidavit that he was the one who grew the produce he had been selling.[150]

Regardless, Chinese vegetable peddlers seemed to be quite popular. In fact, on Saturday, March 20, 1886, the Napa Anti-Chinese League met and passed a resolution demanding that white residents stop patronizing Chinese vegetable peddlers or face repercussions. Part of the resolution reads, "*Resolved*, That the members of the League who are so patronizing Chinese vegetable peddlers be requested to immediately stop such patronage, and in case they refuse, their names be read in open meeting, and that they remaining members of the League proceed to boycott them strictly and with determination."[151] In Calistoga, the local newspaper declared that "[n]o more is the Mongolian vegetable peddler seen upon our streets. They have been driven out by boycott." They seemed to realize that the peddlers were providing a service that still needed to be filled, as they followed this statement with, "An opportunity now presents itself for some white man, with a team, to peddle from door to door."[152]

An editorial in the *Napa County Reporter* in 1890 declared that there were three hundred Chinese vegetable peddlers in Los Angeles and that it was part of a conspiracy to "freeze" the white farmer out of the business and maintain a monopoly on the vegetable peddler trade.[153] Unsurprisingly, the ugly talk around Chinese vegetable peddlers resulted in anger against them and even violence. Mr. H. Cavagnaro attacked and struck a Chinese peddler several times in front of his Napa hotel in 1885 because he did not like the prices he was asking.[154] In St. Helena later that same year, a white laborer was cutting across a melon patch owned by Ah Sing when he was confronted by Sing for trespassing. The laborer pulled out a pocketknife and "cut the owner of the garden in the right side inflicting a dangerous wound." The attacker left for the Rutherford train station and escaped to San Francisco, where he remained at large.[155] All was not always negative for Chinese vegetable peddlers, however. The *St. Helena Star* in 1887 reported that Chan Ah Lai, a Napa vegetable peddler, "has recently taken unto himself a bride, having married Miss Ling Lee of San Francisco."[156]

While it is tempting to focus on the impact Chinese workers had on the early wine industry in the Napa Valley because it is such an economic success story today, Chinese workers were deeply involved in many industries in the Napa Valley as either the dominant labor contingent or comprising a substantial proportion of the labor force. The Chinese were the main labor force in viticulture, hop farming, railroad construction, domestic servants, cooks and the laundry business in the late nineteenth century. They also formed a significant portion of the general farm and construction laborers, tannery workers and quicksilver miners in the Valley. The success of the entire economic ecosystem of everyone in the Napa Valley was dependent on the Chinese worker.

Chapter 4

CHINATOWNS

Many cities throughout California had Chinatowns that formed an informal network for the Chinese working throughout the state. Every town in the Napa Valley had a region called Chinatown, but the character and relationship of a Chinatown to its surrounding town varied widely even within this relatively small area. The more urban town of Napa had a relatively positive relationship with its Chinatown much of the time, even though it was wholly contained within Napa city limits. Yet more rural St. Helena's Chinatown, which was on the outskirts of town, was a constant source of aggravation to many townspeople. In addition, Yountville, Rutherford, Oakville and Calistoga all had areas that were denoted as Chinatowns by residents.

NAPA

There were several significant Chinese communities within Napa. They were all within a mile or so of a single central area called Chinatown, which was on a small peninsula that was formed at the intersection of Napa Creek as it flowed into Napa River. Winter rains sometimes flooded the riverbanks, and the overflow would flow into Napa Creek, making Chinatown a temporary island. The 1880 census refers to Chinatown by the term "Chinese Island," although it is unlikely that it was actually an island on June 19, 1880, when the census was taken, but rather isolated on two of its sides by water. Maps of the time refer to it as Chinatown.

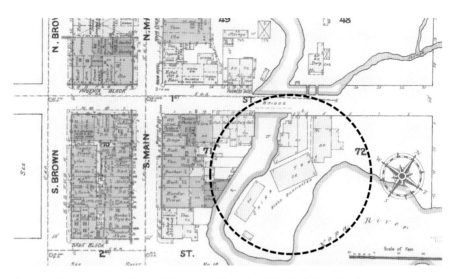

Sanborn Fire Insurance Map of downtown Napa in 1891, including the downtown Chinatown area.

The 1880 census enumerates 60 Chinese residents of Chinatown, or "Chinese Island."[157] Yet it was not even the largest concentration of Chinese people in Napa. There were 98 Chinese workers living in a dormitory (or some other communal living situation) sponsored by the Central Pacific Railroad. There were 65 Chinese workers in the boardinghouse on Grant Avenue next to Sawyer's Tannery,[158] and 27 Chinese people lived in a boardinghouse off Second Street that was designated in the Census as "China Alley." There were even 21 Chinese people classified as "insane" residing at the Napa State Hospital. Given there were 455 Chinese people in Napa, this left 184, or 40 percent of the entire Chinese population, dispersed throughout Napa, either living on their own or within white townspeople's houses as servants or cooks.

TABLE 2. DISTRIBUTED CHINESE POPULATION CENTERS IN 1880 NAPA

Location	*Population*	*Percentage of Total*
Railroad House	98	22%
Tannery House	65	14%
Chinatown (Chinese Island)	60	13%
Chinese Alley	27	6%

Location	Population	Percentage of Total
State Hospital	21	5%
Other	184	40%
Total	**455**	**100%**

Source: U.S. Census Forms for City of Napa, Napa County, 1880.

The area on which Napa's Chinatown was located was called Cornwell's Addition. That area was owned by George Cornwell, a city supervisor and state assemblyman.[159] The Chinese leased the land from him starting in 1852. Early records mention a general store, barbershop, gambling house and opium den. Many of the buildings were built on stilts due to frequent flooding. White townspeople patronized the stores in Chinatown or to try their luck at the various gambling houses.[160]

Suey Ping, the daughter of one of Chinatown's leading merchants, Chan Wah Jack, thought that Chinatown had a population of close to five hundred, but that seems unlikely given the relatively small area of Chinatown and a census tally in 1880 of sixty, even accounting for a census undercount. Regardless, Chinatown seems to have been bustling with activity from Chinese and white townspeople during the day and likely swelled with shoppers and visitors. It was even described as "humble though picturesque" as it looked out over the Napa River.[161]

Napa's Chinatown was largely peaceful and generally had a positive relationship with the broader city. Even an attempted exposé by the *Napa Register* in 1884 was relatively mild. In a front page article titled "CHINATOWN Scenes by Day—How the Night Is Spent—Gambling and Opium Smoking," the *Register* sent a reporter to describe what goes on in Chinatown during a typical twenty-four-hour period. The daytime in Chinatown was quiet and peaceful, the article said, except for the noise from the Chinese laundries. It stated that "here and there small retail shopkeepers offer for sale diminutive pieces of cocoanut [*sic*], sweetmeats, prepared after China fashion and other edibles. Their sales are not large. From different rooms comes the sound of the highly enjoyable native fiddling." Nighttime was supposed to be a different story. However, one of the first complaints was that the laundries were still noisy with Chinese laundrymen working until midnight ironing and cleaning clothes. This 'round-the-clock work ethic was a contributing reason why Chinese-owned laundries kept outperforming their white-owned counterparts.

Late 1800s sketch of the city of Napa. Chinatown is in the center, on the peninsula between Napa River and Napa Creek along First Street. *Online Archive of California, C.J. Dyer, artist.*

Pencil sketch of Napa's Chinatown along the Napa River in 1927 by artist A.E. Burbank.

Fragments of stoneware vessels found along the Napa River bed at the site of Napa's Chinatown. *From the Napa Valley Museum.*

Alan Shepp's mosaic fountain at the Historic Napa Mill downtown contains a panel depicting the 1902 Napa Chinatown Fire. *Author's collection.*

Fires were a constant source of danger to the wood-framed Chinatown buildings. A devastating fire in 1902 destroyed "nearly all the buildings in Chinatown." Only a few small buildings near the creek and the temple, known as a Joss House,[162] were saved from burning. Mrs. Cornwell, George's widow, still owned the land and two of the buildings in Chinatown, but Chinese proprietors owned all the other buildings. The value of the Chinese-owned buildings destroyed by the fire was valued at $4,000, and the building owners vowed to rebuild.[163] By that point, however, the Chinese population was declining, and by 1927, the site had been razed to make way for a yacht harbor, which was never constructed.

Napa's Chinatown was an integral part of a colorful downtown. White and Chinese townspeople frequented the shops, and there seemed to be very little agitation directed toward Chinatown. The peaceful coexistence is likely due to the comparatively small Chinese population relative to the larger town of Napa and the fact that Chinatown was tucked behind Napa River and Napa Creek and out of sight of locals who did want to venture there. The situation was very different in St. Helena, just twenty miles north of Napa.

The Story of Chan Wah Jack, Napa Chinatown Entrepreneur

Chan Wah Jack was born in a Chinese village called Hong Hay Li in 1848. He arrived in Napa in 1860 at the age of twelve to work with his elder brothers, who already owned and operated a Chinese store named Sang Lung. In 1879, he married a woman named Lum from Weaverville, California, and they had two sons, Quock Horn and Wing.[164] Weaverville was the site of a large Chinatown that had an impressive, beautiful temple. Wah Jack remained in Napa until 1883, when he decided to return to China and raise his family, like Jue Joe had done. The rising anti-Chinese sentiment encouraged by the 1882 Chinese Exclusion Act may have contributed to his desire to raise his family in China. He and his growing family remained in China for fifteen years and added two more sons and one daughter. The youngest son, Shuck, was born in 1895.

In 1898, he decided to return to Napa with his family and continue his career as a merchant. The trip back to Napa was perilous. On the voyage back to America in the Pacific Ocean, his ship caught fire, and all the passengers, including three-year-old Shuck, had to evacuate to lifeboats in case their ship would sink. Fortunately for the Chan family, the ship was spared major damage, and they were able to continue their voyage.

He took over running his brothers' Sang Lung Chinese Store in 1898. That store was considered an oasis for homesick Chinese workers who were toiling in the vineyards, tanneries and quicksilver mines. They would visit Wah Jack's place to feel like they were back home. Shuck recalled that they would do deliveries via horse and wagon up and down the Napa Valley and would see Chinese laborers building rock walls, fences and bridges. The rocks weighed as much as five hundred pounds each and had to be wrestled into place by hand. He also remembers Chinese workers visiting Napa's Chinatown on the weekends to drink and gamble.

Chan Wah Jack, like all Chinese residents, faced challenges. He was assaulted in 1904 by a local man named Julius Banchero in front of his Lai Hing store. Banchero was arrested and eventually sentenced to ninety days in jail, but as was common, the judge suspended the sentence if Banchero promised to be on his best behavior. The judge warned that he "would be shown no mercy if he was caught in such a case again."[165] The immediate forgiveness of sentences for crimes was a common practice for white people caught assaulting Chinese residents.

Chan Wah Jack's longevity as a Chinatown merchant and his large and prosperous family led him to be well respected throughout Napa. He and his wife eventually had fourteen children, many of whom went on to have successful careers in the United States, which was a significant accomplishment given the extensive anti-Chinese sentiment at the time.[166] Wing, the eldest son, was a lawyer and was the first Chinese person to be admitted to the California bar.[167] Quock Horn, the second son, married a woman from China who was part of the extended Chinese "royal family." When they had a baby girl in Napa in 1909, it was celebrated throughout

Chan Wah Jack and some of his children in front of the temple in Napa's Chinatown. The photograph was taken on February 19, 1896. *Courtesy of the Napa County Historical Society.*

Napa's Chinatown, as she was the first "Chinese child born in this city of an American-born parent."[168] Shuck invested in restaurants across the United States; Moe had a government job in Alameda, California; and Suey Ping, a daughter, was an honors graduate from both Napa High School and the University of California and worked in higher education in both Napa and China.[169]

Chan Wah Jack was called the "Mayor of the local celestial quarter" by the *Napa Journal* and was considered a "well-known pioneer Chinese merchant" throughout town.[170] When he died in 1922, people acknowledged that his accomplishments and reputation enhanced the relationship between the townspeople of Napa and its Chinatown. The ability and freedom of a merchant who owned his own store, and thus not subject to anti-Chinese action by his employers, allowed him to prosper.

St. Helena

Chinese workers in St. Helena settled in an area south of town, yet outside of town limits, as early as 1868. However, as more Chinese moved into the Valley and the town of St. Helena expanded, the physical distance between locals and the Chinese shrank and tensions increased.[171] John Gillam, a local property developer, bought the land where Chinatown resided in the late 1860s. It was near a gravel pit owned by the railroads where many Chinese laborers worked. He began constructing houses for the Chinese laborers on the land because it seemed convenient for the Chinese and the townspeople. As the population grew, he added structures for even more homes and businesses. Gillam recalled that everyone "was well pleased with the idea of having the Chinatown located in such a favorable place—out of town and away from everyone, and yet close enough so that all could go and see them about work."[172]

As Chinatown expanded, townspeople began to object that it was the first thing visitors traveling north would see as they came into town, and they considered it an eyesore. Exact numbers of Chinese residents are impossible to know, but one estimate is around six hundred; given the total population of St. Helena at less than two thousand, this was a substantial percentage.[173] By 1870, there was a store and a restaurant in Chinatown. By 1884, there was a hotel, multiple stores, an employment office and a temple. There was significant growth, but infrastructure was still rudimentary, with open sewers and animal slaughtering between the shacks.[174]

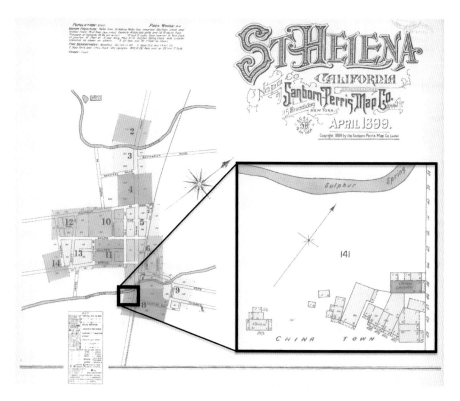

Many St. Helena townspeople hated Chinatown on their southern boundary. They called it the "dingy border of the city" and complained that it tempted the boys and men in town with opportunities for gambling and opium.[175] The three forms of gambling most popular in Chinatown were fan-tan games (similar to roulette), dice games and a daily lottery.[176] Many in Chinatown were poor since they made significantly less than their white laborer counterparts. St. Helena townspeople were getting increasingly agitated at the state of Chinatown and, by extension, its land owner. Gillam defended himself, claiming that he had done St. Helena a favor by refusing to lease any other of his properties in St. Helena to Chinese except for places in Chinatown. He said that the land and buildings in Chinatown represented a large portion of his net worth, and he could not just kick all Chinese out of their homes, despite having "plenty of enemies in St. Helena simply on account of Chinatown."[177] In 1881, townspeople petitioned the town trustees to remove Chinatown because it was "a nuisance, and dangerous to the public health." The city agreed to form a board of health to investigate Chinatown.[178] It took almost three years, but finally the board was incorporated and conducted a formal investigation. It reported that it:

Old St. Helena China Town   - Property of Napa Co. Historical Society

Opposite: 1899 *Map of St. Helena*, showing the location of downtown Chinatown at the southern entrance to the town. *Courtesy Sanborn Fire Insurance Maps.*

Above: Chinatown in St. Helena was a mix of housing and commercial businesses. *Courtesy of the Napa County Historical Society, 1983.16.4.*

found some very foul cess-pools, closets, and drains in the very heart of the town and will recommend stringent measures for their cleaning. Chinatown, as may be surmised, was found to be reeking with filth and bad smells, though the officers state that they were really surprised at the comparative cleanliness of many of these [opium] dens. Tenement houses and pig pens are built side by side and the inhabitants of both are gloriously "mixed."

The board promised to work with some property owners (presumably this just meant John Gillam) to "the best means of abating certain nuisances."[179] While this was progress, it clearly was not what the citizens who petitioned for Chinatown to be torn down had in mind.

In 1884, a large fire destroyed half of St. Helena's Chinatown. The fire raced through the poorly constructed wooden shacks that made up Chinatown, and four stores lost contents valued at $300 through $1,500. The buildings themselves, owned by Gillam, were valued at $1,000.[180] If St. Helena residents thought that would be the end of Chinatown, they were mistaken. Just one week later, Gillam declared that he was rebuilding the burned stores as soon as possible, and the displaced Chinese merchants were already negotiating the lease price to move back in.

The Chinese residents themselves highly valued their Chinatown neighborhood and withstood tremendous pressure to leave, as demonstrated by a twenty-five-year legal struggle to evict them. In February 1886, the simmering tensions between townspeople in St. Helena and Chinatown reached a breaking point. On February 2, two or three hundred "Anti-Coolieites" marched into Chinatown and demanded the Chinese vacate within ten days. The Chinese residents locked themselves in their stores and homes and refused to confront the demonstrators. An editorial in the *St. Helena Star* stated that "Chinatown, particularly in its present location, to be an eye-sore to the town and detrimental to health and good morals and we favor locating it outside the town limits." John Gillam replied that he would be willing to "sell the place at a reasonable figure."[181]

On February 19, 1886, John Gillam sold the land Chinatown was on to the anti-Chinese group in town even though the Chinese Six Companies out of San Francisco had offered $500 more for the property. The *St. Helena Star*

Stoneware pot unearthed near the location of St. Helena's Chinatown. *From the Napa Valley Museum.*

Picture taken at the corner of Main and Charter Oak, just north of Chinatown, 1907. *Courtesy of St. Helena Historical Society.*

happily announced that Chinatown was sold and "[i]ts Moon-eyed denizens must find other quarters."[182] Yet the Chinese residents refused to leave their homes and businesses. The anti-Chinese buyers of the land not only complained that the Chinese would not vacate but Chinatown residents also took the buyers to court to enforce longer-term leases signed by Gillam, including some that went on indefinitely.[183] This legal battle carried on for years, and the Chinese never did vacate their Chinatown neighborhood voluntarily, nor did many of them even pay rent during the proceedings. However, by the late 1890s, their population had dwindled considerably. When a fire consumed the remaining eight buildings in 1911, the anti-Chinese group finally achieved their goal of removing the Chinese from Chinatown, twenty-five years after purchasing the property.[184] The Chinese residents demonstrated remarkable organization, tenacity and knowledge of the legal system for many years to resist eviction.

RUTHERFORD

Several other towns in the Napa Valley had their own Chinatowns, but none of them had the relationship with their towns like the relatively positive experience of Napa's Chinatown or the negative experience of St. Helena's Chinatown. It could be because these Chinatown areas in smaller towns were more transitory in nature than the permanent settlements in Napa and St. Helena. Or it could be that the other towns were so small that they did not have the critical mass to object to their own Chinatowns. Two that are worth examining in some detail were in Rutherford and Calistoga.

Rutherford is a small town about at the midpoint along the north–south axis of the Napa Valley. An early settler there named Florentine (Frank)

Kellogg set up a series of spaced wells and watering troughs in order to encourage riders and stagecoaches to stop on the way up the Valley. In 1871, it got its own train depot and became, for a while, the end-of-track location for the Napa Valley Railroad. It became a focal point for transporting grain and grapes from surrounding areas to more populated areas to the south. Several farms and vineyards were built around Rutherford, and a Chinatown sprang up to house and support the Chinese agricultural laborers working those businesses. By 1881, Ah Gen had set up a Chinese-run laundry that also served as a hiring hall for Chinese farm laborers. In September, he skipped town, leaving behind many unpaid debts.[185] A new manager named Yung Him took over and opened a China Store and a grocery store alongside the hiring hall and laundry. He was ambitious, and by 1884, he had decided to advertise in the *St. Helena Star*, which turned the normally anti-Chinese *Star* into an advocate, at least as long as the advertising dollars kept flowing. It editorialized, "Yung Him, of Rutherford, is an enterprising celestial and advertises his establishment in today's STAR. Such a masterly stroke of business policy is deserving of success."[186] Later that year, he advertised that he could furnish Chinese "grape pickers" for $1.15 per day.[187]

There was very little reporting on the social or economic life of Rutherford's Chinatown. In 1889, the *Napa Register* did report on the investigation into the murder of a Chinese resident of Rutherford named Ah Quan, who was about thirty-five years old. He died from a gunshot wound, but the perpetrator was never found.[188] Rutherford's Chinatown reached a maximum size of about 150 by the end of the 1880s, but it started to shrink soon thereafter. It was razed in 1895 by Thomas Mark, who purchased the land that Chinatown sat on and stated that he would remove all the buildings and build a large and convenient cooper (barrel making) shop.[189]

CALISTOGA

Calistoga's Chinatown was located literally on the wrong side of the tracks from the rest of the town. It was a collection of shacks with low overhanging roofs that provided shelter from the afternoon sun. It was located alongside the Southern Pacific Railroad Depot. Many of the Chinese people who lived there worked as section crews for the railroad. Leila Crouch, the daughter of Charlie Crouch, who worked for the water company in early 1900s Calistoga, recalls the "heavy aroma of incense, which seemed to be burning constantly."[190] One of the most important Chinese-owned businesses in town

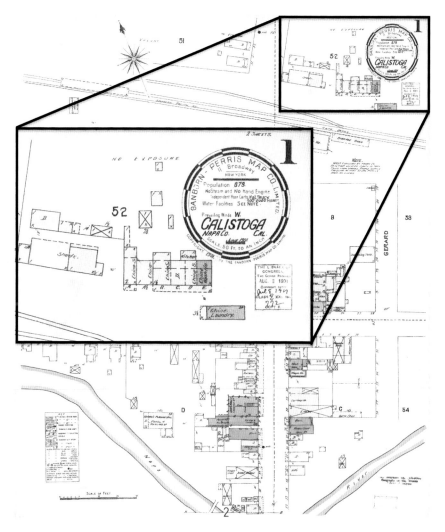

Map of Calistoga in 1901, showing the location of Chinatown at the northeastern edge of town next to the railroad tracks. *Courtesy Sanborn Fire Insurance Maps.*

was Kong Sam Kee's Chinese Laundry and Employment shop. It opened in 1875. Kong Sam Kee was immortalized in Robert Louis Stevenson's travelogue called *Silverado Squatters*. Stevenson was recovering from a chronic respiratory illness and spent a summer in 1880 Calistoga with his family to take in the mountain air. He met Kong Sam Kee because Stevenson was trying to hire a "China-boy" to help with transporting luggage.[191] Kong Sam Kee was a fixture in Calistoga for years.

Calistoga's Chinatown area was the result of a purchase of three acres by S.W. Collins and W.N. Harley in 1883, right beside the Calistoga train depot. They paid $100 per acre with the "intention to give the Chinamen around the country an opportunity to locate there and make an exclusive home for themselves."[192] There is a letter written from Harley to Collins dated October 4, 1896, in which they discuss their Chinatown property, which they still jointly owned. In the letter, Harley wrote that Collins needed to fix "the China Town Roof but get it done as cheap as possible. We can't aford [*sic*] to lose any China men." In addition, it seems there was a bit of a falling out between the two partners, as Harley followed up with "you want to get my half of that property I don't care to sell however you can make me an offer."[193]

Another document from the same general period shows a tabulation sheet of income from rents and expenses for Chinatown during the first part of 1894. Income included rents ranging from $4.00 to $58.00. The total income was $208. Expenses included a $4.75 and a $7.55 allowance back to some tenants for repairs they made themselves and then other expenses for painting ($2.50), white washing ($2.50) and assorted supplies, including $0.25 for the very receipt book that was being used. The net income for the period was $189.55, which was split evenly between Harley and a Mrs. Collins. The financial information and the letter allow for some conclusions regarding Chinatown maintenance. First, Harley and Collins did spend some (though minimal) money maintaining the properties, and they were motivated to keep their Chinese tenants happy enough to stay. Second, the profit margins on the properties were healthy since they pocketed more than 90 percent of the income for the period.

Calistoga's Chinatown did not have a robust commercial area. By 1901, Chinatown had a few laundries and about ten buildings that likely served as housing, gambling establishments or opium dens. However, as with the other Chinatowns in the Napa Valley, Calistoga's could not withstand the demographic changes of the exodus of Chinese residents. In 1914, C.E. Butler, a city labor contractor, purchased the property. The newspaper article describing the sale was almost wistful in documenting the demise of Calistoga's Chinatown:

> *Chinatown in Calistoga will soon be a thing of the past. C.E. Butler has control of the property and is engaged in tearing most of the houses down. The only buildings that have been occupied lately are a store and a laundry. There was a time, about twenty years ago, when Chinatown was a lovely place, but of late years it has been practically deserted.*[194]

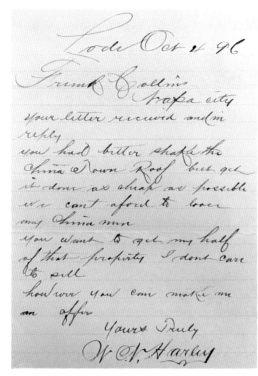

Left: October 4, 1896 letter from W.N. Harley to C.W. Collins discussing the maintenance of Chinatown buildings in Calistoga. *Author's collection, from the Napa County Historical Society.*

Below: Model of Calistoga's Chinatown as displayed in the Sharpsteen Museum in Calistoga. *Author's collection.*

About nine months later, he was almost done clearing the property. As he was tearing down the last few structures, he found a "complete opium smoking outfit" but no opium.[195] Thus, the last of Calistoga's Chinatown was finally erased.

There was some bad blood between residents of St. Helena's Chinatown and Calistoga's Chinatown. Two rival Chinese labor gangs, one from Calistoga and one from St. Helena, were cutting wood on land owned by local resident Charley Loebor. The two gangs had been feuding for a while on the job site. On June 8, 1890, two Chinese labor bosses from Calistoga, Sam Lee and Ah Quey, traveled to St. Helena's Chinatown and entered Ah Kong's store. They saw Quong Mug, the rival St. Helena labor boss, in the back and opened fire with pistols. Quong Mug returned fire, and at least six shots were exchanged. Unfortunately, the only person injured was Ah See, a shopper who just happened to be standing near Sam Lee when the shooting started, taking a bullet to the knee.[196]

Every town in the Napa Valley had its own version of a Chinatown.[197] While they shared some commonalities, such as they all were on land owned by white townspeople who decided, for their own reasons, to allow Chinese people to live and work there, they also had significant differences. Napa's Chinatown was vibrant and seemed to be an integral part of downtown. Both Chinese and white residents of Napa seem to have very fond memories of the "humble though picturesque Chinatown" in their midst.[198] Calistoga and Rutherford both had good relationships with their Chinatowns, but in those cases their Chinatowns were relatively small and mostly residential. St. Helena had an adversarial relationship with its Chinatown due to three factors. First, it was situated at the entrance to town, where it was the first thing that greeted visitors and returning residents alike. In Napa, Chinatown was tucked behind Napa River and Napa Creek and was not in townspeople's normal view if they did not want to see it. In Calistoga, Chinatown was located at the far end of town, next to the railroad tracks, away from residents. Second, St. Helena was a relatively small town with a population around two thousand people. Chinatown had hundreds of residents, so it was quite large relative to the town population and thus likely appeared more threatening. Finally, St. Helena's economy was not as diversified as Napa's, and many of the Chinatown residents worked as vineyard labor, farm workers or miners—all work that St. Helena's white residents presumably could be doing.

Chapter 5

COMMUNITY

The Chinese in Napa were connected to Chinese immigrants all over the West by their language, customs and clan affiliations. All Chinese immigrants in the nineteenth century were from Guangdong Province, Cantonese-speaking people from villages in rice-growing districts along the Pearl River Delta. Canton was their principal city, and they spoke different dialects of Cantonese. Their country was Chung Kou, the "Middle Kingdom," and they knew that they were from a great civilization with a four-thousand-year recorded history. They observed the lunar calendar; believed in Taoism, an indigenous religion; and followed the principles of Confucianism, a philosophy that gave moral order in their daily lives. Family was of primary importance. One's actions reflected one's family and their clan. Their last names came first in identifying themselves. In the villages, their names were recorded in ancestral tables going back thirty generations or more.

The Cantonese had more exposure to the West than the rest of China. In 1757, by imperial degree, Canton was opened as the official port of commerce for China, and until 1840, it was the only major port open to trade with the West. When Chinese workers came in the 1860s, there were already Chinese communities established by merchants. In America, called Gum San (Gold Mountain), there were already organized benevolent associations of people from the same districts in Guangdong, formed for mutual protection and for connection to their villages. Everyone who came to America to work was expected to send part of his wages back to his family.

If a Chinese laborer died working in Gum San, his district association would ensure that he would have a proper burial and his bones be sent back to his village in China. This demand was written in the contract for Chinese workers on the Central Pacific Railroad.

Most Chinese workers were migrant workers. For many of them, there was no stability in their work environment, which could change on them at any moment. The one constant was their family clan, who watched out for them and helped find employment and relayed news from their home village. Traditions from home, including the food they ate, were important to keep up their morale, and they celebrated festivals and holy days with enthusiasm. Significant Chinatowns in the Napa Valley had temples where they could worship and pay their respects. Temples were considered a "home base" and were Taoist with Buddhist symbols and images from Chinese folklore. Stores and gathering places of all kinds invariably had a shrine. There were also Chinese organizations like the Chinese Six Companies and the Chinese Free Masons that provided emotional, social and even financial support. These communal groups would provide a social safety net that would allow the Chinese to remain and be as successful as possible in the Napa Valley.

THE CHINESE SIX COMPANIES

The Chinese Consolidated Benevolent Association, better known as the Chinese Six Companies, was an organization based out of San Francisco that served as the primary advocate for Chinese immigrant workers. It initially comprised members of six districts in China from which most immigrants came. The number of districts, or associations, varied over the years, but the name Chinese Six Companies remained. It would adjudicate disputes among members, promote programs for the welfare of Chinese residents and fight anti-Chinese legislation at the city, state and national levels. The leadership of the Chinese Six Companies would rotate each year so that no one district could dominate the others.

In addition to aiding Chinese while they were in California, the Chinese Six Companies also helped immigrants pay for their passage to California. While some were able to pay for their own passage to America or were helped by family already there, many potential émigrés could not afford transportation. The Chinese Six Companies would work out a "credit-ticket" system where it would pay for the immigrant's passage to San Francisco. The Chinese Six Companies would then house them temporarily in San

Francisco, get them any needed medical care and then help them find work in the Napa Valley or elsewhere.[199] In return, the worker would repay the Six Companies over time until the cost of transportation was paid off, which could take anywhere from two to five years.[200]

Even laborers who did not borrow from the Chinese Six Companies for transportation, like Jue Joe, still benefited from the Six Companies to get oriented in California and find work, as he did first in Marysville and then in St. Helena. Ezekiel B. Vreeland, U.S. deputy commissioner of immigration from 1873 to 1876, estimated that 80 percent of all Chinese immigrants to California were brought in by the Chinese Six Companies.[201] They also provided legal support to challenge anti-Chinese laws, such as when Sam Kee challenged a discriminatory laundry ordinance passed by the City of Napa.

CHINESE FREE MASONS

Many Chinese men in the Napa Valley were active in the "Chinese local lodge of Free Masons," also known as the Chinese Masonic Lodge, Chinese Free Masons or Zhigongtang (Chih-kung t'ang). The Zhigongtang, which means "Active Justice Society," was a secret society established in 1674 in the Guangdong and Fujian Provinces in China. They were founded in opposition to the Manchu Qing Dynasty, which ruled China from 1644 to 1912. In response to the anti-Manchu Taiping Rebellion from 1850 to 1864, many Taiping supporters fled overseas and started Zhigongtang secret societies, including one in San Francisco in 1853. Newspapers in San Francisco investigated the Zhigongtang, and even though it sought to overthrow the Qing Dynasty in China, they found nothing objectionable in its presence in the United States and said it was like the Masonic or Odd Fellows fraternal organizations. Zhigongtang leaders liked that association and called themselves Chinese Free Masons to align themselves in the public's mind with the European/American Free Mason organization of George Washington and Benjamin Franklin. Between the 1870s and 1890s, almost every major Chinese American community had a Chinese Free Mason branch, including the communities in the Napa Valley.[202]

The organization tailored itself to local environments but generally embraced a self-supporting fraternal brotherhood ethos. All initiates into the Chinese Free Masons had to agree to thirty-six oaths, including loyalty to the other "brothers" in the organization, to not inform on their new brothers, to share one's wealth with brothers, to not steal from a brother, to live in harmony and to not share secrets of the organization with outsiders. They had to help one another, whether they were rich or poor.[203] In 1884, thirteen Chinese men were initiated as Free Masons in St. Helena's local courtroom, as no hall in Chinatown was big enough to host the numerous dignitaries who attended the ceremony, including forty Chinese Masons from San Francisco. There were celebrations in St. Helena's Chinatown of firecrackers, gongs and a huge feast to commemorate the occasion.[204] Later in 1884, the *Napa Reporter* wrote that there was an initiation of new members in the Napa chapter of the Chinese Masonic Lodge, which was organized recently by Chinese residents in Chinatown.[205]

The Chinese Free Mason organization grew throughout the late nineteenth century and was wealthy enough to aid in building temples in Chinatowns. The construction of the temples, called "Joss Houses" by white townspeople, was a significant milestone in the maturation of a Chinese community and was celebrated by surrounding Free Mason groups. In 1890, the temple in Napa during a Chinese New Year's celebration was described as follows: "The public Joss-house, nicely fitted up, with an open side, fronts on the river. Before the image of the Joss are offerings of rice, meats, oranges, candy, cocoanuts [*sic*] and other Chinese delicacies. The floor is covered with matting and rugs and the walls in the house are papered."[206]

The first report of plans for a temple in St. Helena's Chinatown came in June 1884.[207] The establishment of a temple indicated a significant commitment to the local community of Chinese residents. It took a long time for the St. Helena temple to be completed. Plans for the temple were drawn up by John Gillam, the owner of the Chinatown land. Seven years later, the construction was undertaken by the Mixon & Son construction company.[208] The St. Helena temple was completed in October 1891 and resulted in a weeklong celebration in Chinatown. The master of ceremonies for the opening event was Sam Sing Lung, who was a high-ranking official in the St. Helena Chinese Free Masons. A Chinese band was brought up from Napa to play at the ceremony. On the altar in the temple was a "gold-mounted idol in the shape of a dragon" and four bronzed vases and burning incense. The idol and vases cost the Free Masons $100. The cost of the entire building and furnishings was $5,000, which demonstrates both the wealth of the Chinese Free Mason organization and how important the temple was to the community.

Sam explained the membership process to the Free Masons. "Those desiring to join the lodge," he said, "had to send in their names and remain on probation for three months, at the end of which time they were admitted to membership, if they were found to bear a good character, otherwise they were excluded." The initiation fee was scaled to meet the income level of the new member. In 1891, there were between five hundred and six hundred Chinese Free Masons in Napa County, which would have represented more than half the Chinese residents in the county.[209] The Free Mason organization was very likely the most powerful, wealthy and influential formal organization that most of the Chinese men in the county interacted with on an ongoing basis.

FUNERALS, BURIALS AND THE AFTERLIFE

One of the important functions the Chinese Free Masons performed in the Napa Valley was funerals and burials. Back in China, funerals were handled by family members. But since the vast majority of the Chinese in the Napa Valley were without family, the Free Masons provided this necessary and important service. Part of the annual dues paid to the Free Mason organization was a "death insurance fee." Very specific funereal rites and rituals had been important to Chinese culture for centuries. One of the key oaths of the Zhigongtang back in China was oath no. 23: "Everyone should wear mourning for his parents or relative for three years. During this period he should not behave improperly. Those who break this law will be sentenced to die at Shao Yang Mountain." The funeral process in China involved extended family members performing duties like preparing the body for burial and dressing it in the deceased's finest clothes, being part of the funeral processional and standing at the grave site wishing the deceased best wishes as he traveled to the afterlife.[210]

This process could not be followed by the Chinese laborers in California and the Napa Valley because they almost never had family around. The Free Masons assumed the role of family and made other adjustments to account for the reality of being in a foreign land, like advising that proper mourning behavior be followed for at least three months, not three years. Important aspects of the process that remained unchanged were the public procession through town to the grave site and the constant presence of music. Loud noises and scattered paper with holes were thought to scare off any evil spirits that might follow the procession. If Chinese musicians could not be found, American musicians would be hired to play American music.[211] In the Napa Valley, this was not an issue, as there were Chinese bands in Napa and nearby San Francisco, so Chinese music could always be played.[212] The public nature of Chinese funerals gave locals a chance to observe and interact with Chinese residents in a way that the two groups, mostly segregated, did not often experience.

In 1884, a wealthy St. Helena Chinese businessman had died of consumption, and a long funeral procession wound through town led by a carriage containing a Chinese band of "three cymbals, a horn and a drum." This was followed by the hearse, fifty to seventy-five Chinese marching two abreast and finally a carriage containing four of the leading merchants of Chinatown.[213]

In 1899, Wong Chow Tuck's funeral was considered the "greatest Chinese funeral ever held" in Napa. Every carriage in town was seemingly employed in the funeral procession as it wound its way from Tuck's house on Pearl Street past Chinatown and on to the cemetery. Two professional mourners were brought in to augment the service, and Kong Sow, a San Francisco Confucian priest, officiated the ceremony.[214]

A St. Helena resident named Lea Hau, aged fifty-three, was working in Rutherford with five other Chinese workers cutting down trees when he slipped trying to run away from a falling eucalyptus and was crushed to death. His funeral was put on by the Chinese Free Masons two days later in St. Helena's Chinatown. The funeral procession from Chinatown to the grave site wound through town. It consisted of a Chinese band at the start of the procession right after the hearse and a wagon full of food for the ceremony and was followed by fifty Chinese marchers, ten vehicles and another Chinese band bringing up the rear. The modified graveside ritual put on by Free Masons was reported by the *St. Helena Star* the following day and included the following:

> *Matting was placed along side the grave and on this the edibles were spread. Two of the order stepped forward, bowed three times, sank on their knees, bowed three times again, took up small vessels filled with gin, spilled it on the grade and rose with bows, making room for the next. About five or six couples went through this performance, when it seemed to occur to them it would be quicker to get a large number, so about twenty went through the ritual at once. Then the High Priest, with basket in hand, held a short oration joined in with a chorus from all the Chinese present. After gathering up the edibles they left for Chinatown where we presume the mourners feasted.*
>
> *During all this time a number of Chinese lighted many candles and other incense, and were kind enough to distribute some on each grave. They*

kept a good fire of papers covered with Chinese characters while the grave was being filled by the sexton. Taking all in all a Chinese funeral is quite an interesting affair.[215]

The reporting from the normally anti-Chinese *St. Helena Star* about the process was surprisingly muted and respectful. Many of the Chinese who immigrated to the Napa Valley during this period were worried about receiving a proper funeral and thus wanted to return to China to be appropriately buried. Some were exhumed and returned, but many, with the aid of the Free Masons–directed appropriate funerary rites, could rest easy knowing that they were given a proper burial in their adopted country.[216]

Tulocay Cemetery was founded in Napa in 1859 and continues to this day to serve as the town's main cemetery.[217] Nearly one hundred Chinese residents of Napa were buried in Tulocay in the late 1800s and the early 1900s. Between 1884 and 1902, eighteen Chinese graves were removed and shipped back to China, which means most of the Chinese residents of Napa buried in Tulocay made it their final destination.[218] There is an area of the cemetery known as the "County Section" where many deceased Chinese were buried. In this section, only seven stone markers put up by wealthier Chinese residents still remain. Less prosperous Chinese had wooden markers, which have long since burned or decayed. Since the specific location of those graves is now unknown, no further burials are allowed in that section.

The marble headstones are interesting for what they choose to tell us. Six of the seven headstones have both English and Chinese writing on them, but they weren't word-for-word translations. The English terms were limited to the person's Anglicized name and English birth and death

Three of the seven remaining headstones at the "County Section" in Tulocay Cemetery in Napa. *Author's collection.*

Remaining markers in Chinese Potter's Field in St. Helena Cemetery are very small and nondescript. *Author's collection*.

dates. The Chinese letters not only included Chinese equivalent dates with a reference to the emperor but also provided context on the village or area the person was from in China, demonstrating the importance of the worker's home village.

The St. Helena Cemetery included at least forty-three Chinese graves. They were all buried in the area of the cemetery known as "Chinese Potter's

Field." Normally, a potter's field in a cemetery would refer to a location for unknown or indigent people. In this case, it seems to serve more as a location for all Chinese in the cemetery, regardless of their economic or social status. Sadly, most of the grave markers were washed away during a flood in the 1930s, but there are a few small markers remaining. Unfortunately, the remaining markers are small and nondescript.

The records at St. Helena Cemetery, which may be incomplete, indicate that of the forty-three Chinese people buried there, four were women and thirty-nine were men. Three of the four women were married, and eight of the thirty-nine men were married. The Chinese buried here came mostly from St. Helena and Rutherford, but some were also from Oakville or Napa. At least seven were disinterred and their remains sent back to China, all in 1913. The earliest burial is from 1879, a twenty-eight-year-old married woman named Mock Yan. The latest burial is from 1939 for an eighty-nine-year-old man, also married, named Ah Joe. We also have the causes of death for the deceased, which are mostly listed as heart disease, pneumonia and tuberculosis—likely the same causes one would see in any other section of the cemetery for people buried in the same period.

TEMPLES AND SHRINES

The three primary religious belief systems of the Chinese that came to California in the 1800s were Taoism, Confucianism and Buddhism. The temples where Chinese worshiped that were established in the Napa Valley, called "Joss Houses" by locals, were almost always described as Taoist. Taoism was a belief based on the doctrines of a sixth-century philosopher named Lao-tse. He believed in simplicity, freedom from materialism and the harmony of man and nature. Taoists also believed in saints, and they worshiped many different gods. Their places of worship, the temples, evolved into ornate buildings with pictures of many different deities.[219] Some were believed to be wrathful and some benevolent and caring. Good spirits were to be thanked but not feared. Evil spirits, on the other hand, must be supplicated and kept in good humor by presents and attention. This explained the constant presence of incense and offerings in temples throughout the Napa Valley.[220]

In addition to dedicated temples, most buildings had a shrine. The *Napa Register* noted that in Chinatown, "every room, be it store, opium den, or gambling nook, there are in secluded corners inscriptions in large Chinese characters, before which are continually burning tapers, to propitiate evil spirits or to bring good luck."[221] The most popular of all figures in the shrines was Guan Gung, a folk hero who was a general, who was often called a god of war but was more commonly revered as a god of righteousness. He was an important figure for merchants because he was known to be just and fair. His image gave workers encouragement to be brave, true and steadfast.

In 1884, Chan Wah Jack and several other Chinese residents decided that Napa's Chinatown needed a temple. They completed it in 1886, and it was named the Bei Di (God of the Big Dipper) Temple. The Chinese Free Masons donated funds for the construction of the temple and for an ornate altar, which was decorated with elaborate carvings and covered with gold leaf. The temple was subsequently used as a meeting hall for the Free Masons.[222] When Napa's Chinatown was razed in 1929 for a proposed yacht harbor (which was never built), Shuck Chan, Chan Wah Jack's son, rescued the altar from the temple before it was destroyed and stored it in a warehouse he owned. In 1964, he donated the altar to the Chinese Historical Society of America in San Francisco, where it remains today.

The altar was covered with poems that were deeply spiritual. Lee Liu Chin, cofounder of the Chinatown History and Cultural Association, described the Napa Chinatown altar as follows:

The poems engraved on this beautiful altar have great significance for the Chinese immigrants who visited the temple. The words reflect the spiritualism of Taoism, the veneration of nature and the supernatural, which is a belief ingrained in Chinese culture for thousands of years. The writings are beyond simple translation, but they evoke the image of infinity and realms beyond realms. This particular shrine is purely Taoist, without Buddhist symbols or any images from Chinese folk culture. Shrines like this one were in temples throughout the west coast from the late 1800s to early 1900s and gave Chinese workers and their families comfort, inspiration, and the will to endure.[223]

In 1877, Reverend Augustus W. Loomis described the morality of Chinese immigrants before a Senate subcommittee:

There is a religious feeling in China which prompts them to give for the support of benevolent institutions. They expect merit from it; and the same thing prompts them in the saving of life. They will risk their own lives to save the lives of those who fall into the river or are drowning. I have seen that myself. They expect merit from it…the degree of knowledge is

The altar was moved from the Joss House before Napa's Chinatown was destroyed and eventually donated to the Chinese Historical Society of America in 1964. *Courtesy of Connie Young Yu.*

universal; to be a scholar is the highest honor, and opens the way to office and to advancement in every respect.

The classics are taught in the schools, also books of proverbs. These proverbs are committed to memory, and become perfectly familiar to the people, high and low. Mottos, proverbs, and moral maxims are posted up in every house and shop, and in every room in every house; the children become familiar with them and these maxims and speeches of their sages, and rules for an upright and virtuous life, go with them wherever they wander over the face of the earth.[224]

Despite the moral and spiritual philosophy of the Chinese workers, some in Napa's Christian community were still interested in converting the "heathen" Chinese. In 1883, the Board of Foreign Missions raised $400 to purchase an old brick church in downtown Napa on Franklin Street that was formerly a Baptist church. It was about four blocks from Chinatown. The board spent an additional $200 to have it re-roofed and repainted inside and outside and named it the Chinese Mission Chapel. After it was dedicated by Reverend A.J. Kerr of the Chinese Mission in San Francisco, it was turned over to the First Presbyterian Church in downtown Napa for ongoing operations. The *Napa Register* thanked the church leaders for "the success that has attended his efforts in this line of Christian warfare."[225]

Not everyone in town liked the addition of a religious building dedicated to converting Chinese to Christianity. Two weeks after it opened, a gang of between thirty and forty boys and young men, led by a twenty-four-year-old named A. Littleton, marched through town to the front door of the chapel. When the door was opened, the group threw rocks and other small projectiles at the building and the people inside. The group was eventually frightened off, and because disturbing a religious program was a misdemeanor, law enforcement got involved; fifteen of the gang were arrested and punished with fines ranging from three to fifteen dollars.[226]

The organizers and supporters of the chapel were not deterred, and a year later, it hosted a Chinese New Year celebration that contained songs in both English and Chinese, accompanied by a Chinese organist, Wah Lee. The sermon was given by Mr. Ling in Chinese and then by Reverend Richard Wylie and Professor D.W. Hanna in English.[227] Later in 1884, the Sunday school run out of the Chinese Mission Chapel was averaging twenty students per week.[228] In 1889, it was the scene of a Chinese New Year's celebration that was "crowded almost to suffocation." It featured Chinese students who sang songs, spoke and served refreshments to all those assembled.[229]

CHINESE HOLIDAYS AND FESTIVALS

There were many propitious days in the lunar calendar observed religiously by Chinese in America. They practiced what they learned from their childhood in their villages. The most important holiday was the celebration of the lunar new year. New Year's Eve was a special day for kinfolk to gather and share a vegetarian meal to cleanse the body and spirit followed by feasting the following day. While there were numerous celebrations throughout the Napa Valley, many workers would go to San Francisco, where they had their family association, for more elaborate festivities. The celebration of the lunar new year would last for several days at least, with lion dances to chase away evil spirits; larger communities would see an elaborate dragon with a procession all could join, banquets in restaurants and street performances and opera.

Chinese opera performances took place early in San Francisco's Chinatown, where there were two established opera houses in the 1870s. Traveling opera companies went to larger Chinese communities throughout California, notably Weaverville, Marysville and Stockton. The Chinese workers knew the performances by heart. Cantonese opera is characterized by singing, simple staging and elaborate costumes and makeup. Women's roles were performed by men. Most popular were performances of the *Romance of the Three Kingdoms*, a classic Chinese historical story rendered in opera. The greatest hero was Guan Gung, a general in Chinese history, who exemplified truth and justice and was revered as a god. Statues of him were popular in temples and were also placed in Chinese stores as symbolizing righteousness and honesty. Opera was intended for everyone. In San Francisco, even the poorest worker could go to a performance after a certain time in the night for a reduced price.

In addition to New Year celebrations, there were several other important holidays and festivals for local Chinese throughout the year. Ching Ming, meaning "bright and clear," is a traditional spring festival when Chinese would go to the tombs of their ancestors and bring food offerings—most importantly a roast pig—and light incense and have a feast at the grave sites. In the Napa Valley, the Chinese would have gone to the St. Helena Cemetery and Napa's Tulocay Cemetery to perform the same rituals that their families in China would be doing. The "Feast of the Hungry Ghosts," or All Soul's Day, is a summer festival elaborately celebrated for several days in larger Chinatowns. It is a holiday to feed the lost souls that have no family to placate them. There are strings of firecrackers lit to chase away evil spirits, a lion dance, a procession led by Taoist priests, music performances and feasting.[230] Finally, the Moon Festival, celebrated in autumn, is based on an ancient Chinese legend. It is a joyful festival celebrated with music and the eating of "moon cakes." In September 1883, the *Napa Register* reported that local Chinese residents were celebrating the Moon Festival in Napa's Chinatown and had erected a flagpole that displayed the Chinese flag with a dragon on it.[231]

CHINESE NEW YEAR CELEBRATIONS

The annual Chinese New Year's celebrations were a cause for excitement and merriment for every town in the Napa Valley. Beginning as early as 1878, the annual fireworks demonstrations became known as an event to which everyone looked forward. In St. Helena on February 13, 1880, "Ginger" took out an ad in the *St. Helena Star* that invited the whole town of St. Helena to view "Fire-Crackers" that would be burned in front of his shop in Chinatown in honor of Chinese New Year.[232]

Not everyone in town was pleased about the celebration. A "Captain Gluyas" complained to local authorities in late January 1884 that two dozen of his finest chickens had been stolen on Saturday night, and he was sure that they were plundered by the Chinese getting ready for their New Year's festivities. This apparently was a mildly scandalous tradition in town.[233]

NEW ADVERTISEMENTS.

Chinese
NEW YEAR!

Will be celebrated by a Grand Discharge of Fire-Crackers at the Store of the Quong Loon High Company, Chinatown, next SUNDAY, at FOUR P. M. Citizens generally are invited to witness it.   " GINGER."

"Ginger," a shop owner and labor boss, would invite the public every year to his shop to celebrate Chinese New Year. *From the* St. Helena Star, *February 13, 1880.*

On February 1, 1889, the *St. Helena Star* commented that Chinese New Year's festivities had commenced on Monday of that week and that "Chinatown is now arrayed in holiday attire, and the celestials are enjoying themselves firing crackers and eating China delicacies."[234]

In Calistoga's Chinatown, Kong Sam Kee—of Robert Louis Stevenson's *Silverado Squatters*—won a friendly competition with a fellow Chinese laundryman to see who had the best fireworks to celebrate Chinese New Year in 1884. The *St. Helena Star* reported that Kong Sam Kee "closed his new year festivities with a grand explosion of fire-crackers Saturday evening, his idea being to outdo Sam Sing Lung's recent

Two Chinese men posing at Tubbs Mansion in Calistoga—perhaps during a Chinese New Year celebration. *Courtesy of the St. Helena Historical Society.*

effort. The K.S.K. man made the most noise, and was therefore No. 1."[235] During the 1882 Chinese New Year's celebration in Rutherford, the Chinese laundry, called the Rutherford Washing Company, hosted an open house and invited the public—Chinese and white residents—to partake of cold chicken, brandy, cigars and Chinese delicacies.[236]

The coverage of Chinese New Year celebrations by the local newspapers reflected the general attitude toward the Chinese in their midst. The *Napa Register*, slightly more friendly to its Chinese residents than the *St. Helena Star*, ran a front-page story on February 8, 1889, that provided background on the celebration and how much it meant to the Chinese residents of Napa:

> *A visit to Chinatown is, at this season of the year, full of interest to any one. The Chinese New Year began last Tuesday night and will close next Monday. All the principal stores are decorated with Chinese lilies, paper flowers, lanterns and various ornaments made from brightly colored paper, bearing Chinese characters. During both day and night, for the Celestial sleeps very little during New Year's week, immense lots of fire-crackers are exploded, filling the air with sulphureous [sic] smoke.*[237]

New Year's was the one time each year when the Chinese community explicitly reached out to the entire town to include them in the celebration. In another relatively expansive article by the *Napa Register* in 1880, it stated:

> *Eating, drinking, gambling and smoking occupy the time of each of the one or two hundred Chinamen thus crowded together. Business is for the time suspended, and gifts are freely bestowed, many American families being the recipients of costly presents from their Chinese servants.*[238]

Chinese New Year was even celebrated at the Great Western Mine by the Chinese miners and became a cross-cultural holiday. The white families of the supervisory and support staff "had so large a share in this festival that they came to think of it as one of their own holidays." A diary entry at the time recalls:

> *The Chinamen celebrated their New Years about a week ago. We were well remembered, receiving from different ones about a doz. silk handkerchiefs, a doz. live chickens and a big turkey, with any quantity of oranges, candy, nuts, preserved fruits, American cakes and Old Bourbon & Cigars. They are very generous at such times.*

Families would come from as far away as Middletown in the next valley over to share the festivities with the miners and the other staff at the mine, but because the roads were so treacherous getting up to the mine, the fireworks were set off in the middle of the day so people could travel back home while it was still light out.[239]

FOOD AND DINING

It was of utmost importance for Chinese workers to have their native food at every meal, and central to their diet was rice. The standard greeting of one Cantonese to another was "have you had rice yet?" The food they ate in Gum San was just like the cooking back in their homeland, a dependable connection to what they felt was the world's greatest cuisine. Whenever possible, Chinese ate their meals communally, with each person having a bowl of steamed rice and sharing a variety of accompanying dishes, everything chopped into bite-sized pieces. They used chopsticks and ate out of porcelain bowls.

Rice, dried fish, preserved vegetables, sauces, tea and utensils were all shipped from China to San Francisco and then transported to Chinatowns and worksites. There was a harmony of ingredients in every dish, and food was intended to nourish both body and spirit. Chinese workers in Napa ate exceptionally well—supplementing their diet of rice, dried fish and preserved vegetables with a variety of fresh local produce and pork from nearby farms. On feast days, they had poultry, elaborate vegetarian dishes, delicate cakes and dumplings. There were capable cooks among them, and labor bosses would procure the best possible things to eat.

WOMEN, MARRIAGE AND FAMILIES

There were very few Chinese women in the Napa Valley between 1870 and 1900. The census records list fewer than 10 Chinese women in both 1870 and 1880 compared with 255 men in 1870 and 846 men in 1880. Many of the Chinese men in the Valley were married, but almost all their wives lived in China. Chinese men with families who were poor enough to need to immigrate to the United States to make money were expected to return to China and their families at some point.[240] Both Jue Joe and Chan Wah Jack followed this pattern after making their initial wealth in California.

It was common for a Chinese man about to emigrate to marry before he left to ensure a wife would be waiting at home and, with luck, give birth to a male descendent while he was gone. The man's relatives back home would closely watch over the wife. In exchange, the man was expected to regularly send back home a portion of his earnings. Whenever possible, the man would return to China to visit and, very occasionally, return with his wife and family.

The trafficking of Chinese girls and young women for slavery and prostitution by criminal tongs and the presence of brothels in Chinatowns caused an outcry among Christian missionaries as well as the general population nationwide. Politicians condemned the entire Chinese population as immoral, degraded and a threat to America's youth and demanded federal action. The Page Act of 1875, America's first restrictive immigration act, was ostensibly written to prevent the immigration of women brought for "immoral purposes" from any country in Asia, but it was aimed at all Chinese females. It effectively discouraged Chinese wives from coming to join their husbands and having families in America.

Despite the few women who immigrated to California from China, there were occasionally Chinese weddings in the Napa Valley that drew attention from locals. The first that occurred in Napa's Chinatown was in 1885 and involved a "petite Chinese damsel all bundled up." It was of intense interest to many white townspeople, who gathered around to watch:

> *The groom, who is Ah Joe, the Chinese cook on the steamer Caroline, stood ready to receive his blushing, prospective bride, and with much ceremony she was conducted into a room where a short and exceedingly puzzling ceremony was performed. The bride's name we could not learn but the name of her father is Si Bo Hi, a doctor by profession. Ah Joe, it is said, paid $1,000 for his bride who was a resident of San Francisco. Today the "happy couple" will give a banquet in Chinatown.*[241]

While that wedding was newsworthy because of its cultural incongruity, there was a double wedding in St. Helena just a few months later between two Chinese couples that was celebrated as an act of assimilation. There are no details about the names of the couples, only that they "had become sufficiently Americanized to adopt the white man's mode of marriage" outside the courthouse in St. Helena.[242]

Through successful weddings and infrequent immigration of entire families, Chinese children slowly began to appear in the Napa Valley. Between 1870 and 1900, their population of children peaked around 1883, dropped precipitously and then settled into a slowly increasing pattern through 1900 (see Table 7 in the appendix). It is difficult to tell exactly when Chinese boys and girls were allowed to attend public schools, but prior to 1890, in a regular status update by the school district, the numbers of white children of school age (ages five to seventeen) and not yet school age (below five) were announced in the paper; the number of Chinese children was given as one number, regardless of age, and they were specifically noted as not being part of the school system. Starting in 1890, that report listed white, Chinese and Black children in school-age and non–school age buckets, indicating that the school-age Chinese students were likely attending public schools.

Formal education of Napa Valley Chinese immigrants began not with the public schools but with the churches. The Christian Missionary Society in China sent Ah Set Fon to Napa to teach English and religious doctrines to the Chinese residents. He was recalled back to China in 1882.[243] He was replaced, and the Chinese Chapel in downtown Napa, reconstructed and rededicated in 1883, served as a de facto school for Chinese children where they were taught how to read and write, much to the consternation of some in town. Those townspeople believed that "the same amount of interest displayed in looking after the welfare of white boys would accomplish more good than is now resulting from the time and money being spent enlightening the Chinese."[244] It is unclear, however, if any townspeople's taxes were being spent teaching Chinese children. The Chinese Sunday school, held in the chapel, had an average attendance of twenty students, and the parishioners had contributed $25.25 toward the school during the first ten months of 1884 alone.[245]

By 1890, the school at the Chinese Chapel had matured enough to put on a demonstration to family and friends, both Chinese and white, as part of the Chinese New Year Celebration. The program highlighted the skills the Chinese had learned in reading and singing and was modeled after a sermon. The program was an accomplishment for the class that demonstrated at minimum the students had good command of reading and speaking English.

St. Helena had its own Chinese Mission School that had at least seven students, all boys, by 1886. It was sponsored by Mrs. Spencer, the wife of Reverend William C. Spencer. The students presented Mrs. Spencer with a seventy-dollar nickel-plated sewing machine as a thank-you for all she had done with the school.[246]

The Chinese residents of the Napa Valley maintained their cultural identity by joining organizations like the Chinese Free Masons, worshiping at various Taoist temples around the area and celebrating homeland events like New Years and funerary rites. Except for a lucky few, Chinese immigrants, who were almost all men, did not have access to their family. They embraced alternatives, like the Free Masons, to provide a sense of belonging. Presumably all the Chinese immigrant workers wanted to return to China at some point, but we know that many did not; they did their best to make the Napa Valley feel like something familiar and comforting—like home.

Chapter 6

UNEQUAL BEFORE THE LAW

O ccasionally, Chinese residents were well served by the justice system, especially when it came to high-level constitutional issues or challenging local ordinances. They were not accorded the same level of representation or accommodation when dealing with petty or violent crimes either perpetrated on or by Chinese residents. The local newspapers seemed to delight in salacious details about crimes perpetrated by Chinese criminals against white townspeople and Chinese-on-Chinese violence, yet at the same time they could not even be bothered to report the names of Chinese who were victims of crimes. Despite this uneven playing field, Chinese people in the Napa Valley frequently stood up for their rights and used the courts aggressively to achieve justice in some form wherever possible.

HISTORY OF DISCRIMINATION

Prior to 1870, Chinese individuals were not allowed to testify in a California court and were especially vulnerable to crimes of all sorts.[247] In 1854, in the case of *People v. Hall*, the California State Supreme Court ruled that Chinese residents should be placed in the same non-Caucasian classification as African Americans or Native Americans. Consequently, the California Criminal Proceedings Act, which stated that "No black or mulatto person, or Indian, shall be permitted to give evidence in favor of, or against, any white person," was expanded to include Chinese in California.[248] As California chief justice Lorenzo Sawyer said in 1867, the Chinese were put in a position of perpetual victimhood:

> *In the nature of things, it would seem, that the very fact of the existence in our midst of a large class of people, upon whom crimes can be committed without fear of detection or conviction, and, therefore, with impunity, must tend to encourage the commission of crimes upon that class.*[249]

This began to change with the passage of the Federal Civil Rights Act of 1870, which codified into law the language of the Fifteenth Amendment to the Constitution, which gave African Americans the right to vote. Section 16 of the Civil Rights Act included language that extended basic civil rights, including the right to give evidence in court, to all persons, not just citizens, within the United States.[250] Section 16 was inserted into the act specifically to help the Chinese residing in, but not citizens of, the United States. Unfortunately, many California courts continued to prevent Chinese from testifying until the California civil code was finally changed in 1872 to comply with the federal mandates.[251]

After 1872, Chinese testimony may have been allowed, but it was not taken nearly as seriously as testimony from white citizens in many local courts of law. An 1887 *Napa County Reporter* editorial claimed that one thing state courts have learned "to their chagrin and sorrow, it is the utter untrustworthiness of Chinese testimony in criminal cases."[252] As late as 1896, the California Supreme Court had no issue with a prosecutor's argument that "in substance, that the jury should disregard the testimony of all the Chinese witnesses in support of an alibi, as against the testimony of the white witnesses for the prosecution."[253] Against that backdrop of unequal treatment before the law, Chinese people in the Napa Valley had to deal with violence and property crimes from other Chinese, as well as from other people in the community, the best they could.

An illustrative example of the lopsided treatment many Chinese victims received in court occurred in 1887. Justice Smith of Napa was sentencing five young men, who were given the moniker "Browns Valley Boys" by the local press, for lying in wait and then stoning and beating two Chinese men named Ah Jim and Ah Sing. Everyone in the courtroom agreed that Ah Jim and Ah Sing did nothing wrong but walk down the wrong road at the wrong time. They were deeply bruised and "severely beaten," and according to the judge, it was just blind luck that either Chinese man was not killed. Yet during the sentencing, the judge said:

I will say to you young men, that what your motive could have been for this brutal and cowardly conduct, I am not able to comprehend. Surely you have no personal grudge against these peaceable men. To be sure they are Chinamen. I am one of those who wish there was not a Chinaman in the land. But that is not the question. These men are under the protection of the Laws of our country. God made them as he also did us. If they were brute animals, say dogs, you would have no right to chase them down as you have done.

But right after that declaration, the judge dismissed the charges of robbery and assault with a deadly weapon, which would have carried a prison sentence. Instead, he gave them a stern lecture that included, "considering your youth and in the hope that this experience will teach you that the laws of your country must be obeyed," and he vowed to make the sentences as light as possible. Each man was fined twenty-five dollars.[254] It is hard to believe that they would have gotten off so easily if, in fact, they had tormented and beaten two dogs instead of Ah Jim and Ah Sing.

Race was clearly the determining factor in severity of punishment. While it was possible to be subject to a twenty-five-dollar fine for attacking and seriously wounding a Chinese man, if the perpetrator was a white "Browns Valley Boy," the magnitude for a Chinese perpetrator for any crime was much higher. Ah Lee was arrested for stealing two ducks belonging to Mrs. Rohlwing of St. Helena. The ducks were found alive and well in Chinatown, which led to Lee's conviction. For this offense, Ah Lee was sentenced to twenty-five days in jail.[255] It is not hard to imagine the penalty would have been even harsher if the ducks had been killed and eaten. Even so, Ah Lee was forced to go without employment or his freedom for almost a month for an offense that would have been worthy of a minor fine, if anything, if he had been white.

OPIUM

In the early 1800s, the British exported opium to China despite objections of the imperial court, which saw the harmful effects of the drug on their people. The emperor Tao Kuang sent Commissioner Lin Tse-hsu to Canton to stop the trade and ordered a ship carrying opium burned in the harbor. He was a hero to his people, but the British retaliated with powerful warships. China lost the Opium War, 1839–42, and was forced

VICTIMS OF OPIUM!

A REMEDY FOR THOSE SUFFERING FROM the effects of Opium or Morphine is now within the reach of all. The Opium can be suspended at once, without nervous suffering, and a permanent cure can confidently be relied upon. The Remedy, if desired, is sent by express to any part of the country. Address P. O. Box 161, San Francisco.

Newspaper advertisement in the December 9, 1875 issue of the *St. Helena Star* indicates that opium addiction was a widespread and common problem.

to concede Hong Kong as a colony to the British. China was weakened and humiliated; a series of unequal treaties with the West ensued, and the opium trade became well established.

Chinese coming to America were portrayed as addicted to opium, corrupting American society and Chinatowns as havens for opium dens. It was legal to sell opium in the United States and Americans frequently used it to help with a variety of maladies. The image of depraved Chinese luring white youth to opium dens was a stereotype used in the relentless campaign to end Chinese immigration and destroy their communities. In an 1874 editorial railing against Chinese attending school at night to learn English, the *St. Helena Star* characterized its Chinese residents as "punk scented, opium smoking, liver colored infidels, who are not and never will become citizens."[256] For Chinese workers, there was no stigma associated with opium, and many used it at work camps before they went to sleep. It was used in a similar manner as many non-Chinese used liquor, and for most it was non-addictive.[257]

Local newspapers played into this anti-Chinese mindset regarding opium and wrote scathing editorials denigrating the Chinese residents in their midst. In 1880, the *Napa Valley Register* called for a decisive action against opium because the "vile and vicious habit of opium smoking is indulged in by boys of respectable parentage, who visit Chinese haunts for that purpose. Such an evil calls for prompt and vigorous treatment on the part of parents, and for a stringent city ordinance or general statute."[258] The *Napa Reporter* shared a scary and threatening tidbit just a year later: "Educated Chinamen claim that in fifty years Americans will be a nation of opium smokers."[259] In 1882, the *Reporter* decided that it needed to be even more direct in a front-page story:

The opium habit has its victims, and the smoking of the drug—the practice being introduced into this country by the Chinese—has extended into the white population to an alarming degree. In small villages like Napa there are many who have become inoculated with the seductive poison, and its dreadful influence has so disorganized their physical systems as to leave them without the power of will to discontinue smoking the opium pipe.[260]

In December 1880, the City of Napa passed Ordinance No. 98, which prohibited "persons from keeping or visiting any place, house, or room where opium is smoked."[261] The way the ordinance was worded would theoretically apply to both Chinese and white operators of opium dens and any Chinese and white patrons. The reality was that despite the lack of racial qualification within the text of the law, application and enforcement was skewed heavily toward the Chinese. Just a few months after the passage of Ordinance No. 98 in early 1881, the Napa police conducted a raid in Chinatown "for the purposes of 'hauling in' anyone who might be found indulging in the proscribed luxury of opium smoking." Unsurprisingly, despite the newspapers' claims of the number of white men and boys who frequented Chinese opium dens, only Chinese opium smokers were rounded up during the raid. The police raided three opium dens and arrested nine people. Six of them were released with fines of six dollars each, one served three days in jail because he could not pay the fine and one went to trial and was found not guilty. The ninth was charged with running the opium den and faced significantly higher penalties.[262]

In June 1882, Charley Baxter was in an opium den run by Ah Louie in Chinatown. Baxter pulled out a gun and shot at a woman in the den but missed. He was arrested and charged with assault with attempt to commit murder.[263] He was found guilty and sentenced to 60 days in the county jail. Ah Louie was also arrested and convicted of keeping a place where opium is smoked, in violation of Ordinance No. 98. He received a sentence of 150 days in county jail—two and a half times longer than the white Charley Baxter, who tried to kill someone. Ah Louie complained after the verdict that the judge must not have liked him very much, although he knew there was nothing he could do about it.[264]

Later that year, a white opium den owner named Steve Brugehetta was arrested for smoking opium, running an opium den and vagrancy. Brugehetta pleaded guilty, and unlike Ah Louie, who spent five months in jail, Brugehetta was fined ninety dollars and was set free. A white woman named Mrs. Sassanett was also convicted earlier that day for operating a different opium den and living in a house of prostitution. She had to pay a fine of forty dollars before she was set free.[265] Both sentences that resulted in modest monetary fines were at a different magnitude than the five months in jail imposed on Ah Louie for ostensibly the same offense.

St. Helena passed an ordinance in 1885 that was supposed to shut down opium dens in its Chinatown. The following year, Constable James Allison of St. Helena arrested Hoe Chin, Och Lee and Ah Charlie for smoking opium in the city limits; they were sentenced to twenty days in jail each.[266] Calistoga, which was an unincorporated city at that time, could not pass its own laws, and its newspaper bemoaned the fact that it would continue "to see four or five opium dens in full blast, with their attendant destabilizing influences, as they are patronized by more whites than people in general are aware of."[267]

While the local papers tended to emphasize how much opium was harming white residents, opium was troublesome for some in the Chinese community as well. Lem Ah Sing, a Chinese resident of Napa, was found dead in the Napa River behind Chinatown early on a May morning in 1888, just a few hours after he was seen leaving an opium den in Chinatown. The coroner ruled the death a suicide, by virtue of the fact that he drowned as a result of his own deliberate act, caused by "sickness and despondency."[268]

Ironically, after the passage of the 1882 Chinese Exclusion Act, which stopped most Chinese immigration and caused the subsequent decline of Chinese population in California and the Napa Valley, the opium "problem" did not get better—it got worse. By 1882, many white Americans had become addicted, and the legal importation of smoking-opium increased dramatically from 859,889 pounds in the 1880s to 924,908 in the 1890s and then 1,481,686 in the first decade of the 1900s. Law enforcement continued to raid opium dens and publish names of people operating them, but that approach had little effect on opium consumption, which continued to be managed as a legal problem instead of a public health problem that affected people regardless of country of origin.[269]

GAMBLING

Gambling closely followed opium as the vice most closely associated with the Chinese residents of Napa Valley. Gambling of various forms was popular among peasants in China, and it spread to California and the Napa Valley along with the influx of Chinese immigrants. These men were paid in cash on a regular basis. While the Chinese professional gamblers became wealthier, many of the Chinese men who played the games became poorer. This cycle depleted any savings they may have accumulated and extended their stay in the Napa Valley in order to earn more to send back home or return themselves.[270] One of the initial platforms of the Napa Anti-Chinese League in 1886 was, "That our police officers be required to act more vigilantly suppressing opium dens and Chinese gambling games."[271] The local papers made Chinese addiction to gambling a special, even dangerous, kind of vice. They reprinted a story saying that gambling debts incurred by the Chinese were prioritized above everything else a Chinese person owned and that they would sell their children to pay off a gambling debt, while ordinary debts, like to a tradesman, would go unpaid.[272] While untrue, there was no one to rebut such a claim.

At the Great Western Quicksilver Mine, professional "sleek, dainty-handed, city-looking, foppish, Chinese gamblers" would show up regularly right after the miners were paid. The sound of fan-tan games would ring out for hours in the evenings while the miners still had money to gamble. The superintendent of the mine, Frank Rocca, would get so incensed that the miners were gambling that he would occasionally march down to China Camp No. 1 or Brown China Camp brandishing his cane in a futile attempt to drive the professional gamblers out. On May 24, 1891, he confiscated $115 from one gambler. There was so much interest in gambling, however, that the professional gambler would typically slink back into camp to continue the game once Rocca had left.[273]

Gambling was an even bigger issue in the cities. The Napa Board of Trustees passed Ordinance No. 23 in 1880 titled "An Ordinance Relating to the Preservation of the Peace, Quiet, and Good Order of the City of Napa." While it opened with prohibitions on prostitution, indecent exposure and dressing in the clothes of the opposite gender, it included the following section:

> Section 6. No person shall keep or maintain or become an inmate of, or visitor to, or shall in any way contribute by patronage or otherwise to the support of any disorderly house or house of ill-fame or place for the practice of gambling within the limits of the City of Napa.[274]

This ordinance provided the instrument by which the city could roust and close Chinese gambling houses. Just a few months later, the police enthusiastically sought to enforce the order prohibiting gambling, and thirteen Chinese men were arrested and brought to trial for "visiting gambling tables." Two of the accused pleaded guilty and were sentenced. However, the others demanded a jury trial and were acquitted because of an administrative oversight that the trustees had never published the ordinances in the local newspaper.[275] This was rectified four weeks later with the publication of the ordinance.

Like the opium laws, anti-gambling laws were almost exclusively applied to Chinese gambling halls and then only to Chinese patrons within those establishments, despite clear evidence of gambling by white townspeople. It became so one-sided that the *Napa Register* editorialized on the disproportionate application of the law. In February 1885, two deputy sheriffs and two citizen assistants raided a fan-tan house, arrested seventeen Chinese gamblers and confiscated the house pot of fifty dollars. Five were deemed "cripples" or "sick" and were released. The other twelve were arrested and sentenced by the county court. The *Register* questioned whether this unbalanced application of justice helped stop gambling within Napa:

> *Are there not habitual violators of the gambling ordinances, in this city, of Caucasian extraction? If there are such, would it not be more in keeping with the dignity of this great American Republic to set an example for the heathen within the gates of our city by jerking up these white malefactors. If we havn't [sic] the "sand" to make a white man respect the law, we will add but little to our fame by crowding defenseless Chinamen.*[276]

Its editorial fell short of fully endorsing equality before the law or challenging the law as a thinly veiled attack on only Chinese gambling, but it is noteworthy that it called out the city on its uneven application of the ordinance.

The presence of gambling was a frequent criticism of St. Helena's Chinatown by townspeople, who claimed to be worried about the morality of the town's youth. As part of the formation of the town's Anti-Chinese League, the group claimed that "[i]n gambling dens and opium joints, which are ever in secret operation, despite the vigilance of law officers, are hell holes that must necessarily lead the youth of our town into vice to a greater or less extent."[277] St. Helena passed a formal anti-gambling ordinance in 1883 whose goal was to "prohibit and suppress gaming and gambling houses and visiting gambling houses and to prohibit and suppress games of chance in public places, etc. and to prevent immorality."[278]

Less than six weeks later, the police raided a gambling house on Main Street operated by Hop Hung.[279] The police were suspicious because that house was shrouded and dark, while all the surrounding buildings were brightly lit. Two police officers plus a "large posse of citizens" raided the establishment while the games were being played. As many as fifty of the gamblers were able to escape up the stairs and onto the roof, but thirteen were arrested and marched to the county jail, escorted by more than one hundred white townspeople; $95.65 was seized from Ah Shuey, who was the dealer and represented the "house." Other than $41.10 confiscated from one other person arrested, Ah Hoy, the remaining eleven had less than $10 between them.[280] The seizure demonstrates both how popular gambling was if at least sixty men were present in one gambling house and the large economic disparity between the house and the gamblers.

The 1883 St. Helena ordinance may have been intended to reduce immorality by shutting down gambling establishments, but they were still going strong six years later. Unsurprisingly, violence often occurred in the intense atmosphere of the gambling den. In July 1889, one Chinese gambler shot two other Chinese gamblers in Chinatown. One of the Chinese victims, a miner who worked at the White Sulphur Springs Quicksilver Mine, was shot seriously in the left thigh and could not be treated immediately due to all the swelling. The other Chinese victim apparently had been on a bit of a winning streak, as the bullet struck his purse that was full of coins and bounced off, leaving only a deep bruise.[281]

VIOLENT CRIMES

Overall, Chinese laborers had more to fear from injuries and deaths sustained due to unsafe working conditions than as a result of criminal activity, but there were Chinese victims of violent crimes by both white townspeople as well as other Chinese residents. One of the earliest mentions we have of a Chinese victim of a violent crime was in 1875 involving Ah Yung, who was shot to death by his labor boss, a fellow Chinese worker known as Ike. Ike worked for John Gillam, the owner of the land on which St. Helena's Chinatown was built. Ike and his crew did some work for Gillam, and as was customary, Gillam paid the labor boss, who was supposed to dole it out as appropriate to his crew. Apparently, Ike hadn't paid his crew, and Ah Yung confronted Ike, who proceeded to shoot him twice with a revolver, killing him. Ike escaped and was never brought to justice.[282] The story of the killer of a Chinese man escaping and not ever being brought to justice was a common refrain across many of the violent crimes committed against Chinese victims.

Local newspapers typically downplayed (or ignored) Chinese-on-Chinese crime but sensationalized Chinese-on-white crime. A Chinese resident of Yountville assaulted another Chinese man in 1885 and was found guilty and fined $30 or thirty days in jail. No names were provided, and the article was printed in the newspaper in just one sentence after a story of the reorganization of the Oak Leaf Social Club and before a new snippet about overcrowded schools. In 1897, a Chinese cook named Goy Lee assaulted a white coachman named August Stillberg, and that story received a separate article with its own headline and included every available detail. Punishments were similarly based on the race of the victim. Goy Lee, by attacking a white man, had to post a $500 bail versus just paying a $30 fine if he had attacked a fellow Chinese man. The way the two crimes were reported in the newspapers demonstrated that Chinese-on-Chinese crime was so expected and common that you did not even need the names of the people involved in the fight. But Chinese-on-white crime needed to be called out to warn the local citizenry.

One of the most notorious episodes of a Chinese murder victim was an 1894 killing of a Chinese farm laborer by a white transient. It was covered extensively by the local papers. On October 30, 1894, two white transients named Joe Talbert and Charles Weston were walking across a field when they came upon fifteen Chinese laborers working on Lorenzo Carbone's potato field in Napa. Talbert and Weston came up to the Chinese workers and asked for a match, and when refused, they continued to pester the Chinese workers. One of the workers, Yeg Chum, told the men to leave. The men, in

---

—The Napa Ladies' Seminary opened to-day with a flattering promise of a pleasant and successful term.

—A number of the old members of the defunct Oak Leaf Social Club are taking steps towards the re-organization of that club.

—The Yountville Chinaman who assaulted another heathen at that place, the other day, was found guilty and fined $30 or thirty days in jail.

—The primary departments of the Napa public schools, in three separate buildings, are uncomfortably crowded with youngsters; the rooms seat about 60 on an average.

Assaulted by a Chinaman.

Tuesday afternoon J. B. Atkinson's coachman, August Stillberg was assaulted and badly wounded by the cook, a Chinaman named Goy Lee, being struck on the head either by a pistol or a stick of wood. The injured man was brought to town where his injuries were dressed. Wednesday he swore to a warrant and Goy Lee was arrested on a charge of assault with intent to commit murder. Justice Chinn released him on $500 bail and the preliminary examination will be held next Tuesday.

Newspapers reported news about Chinese violence quite differently depending on who was attacked. *From the January 16, 1885* Napa Register *(left) and May 28, 1897* St. Helena Star *(right).*

turn, saw Yeg's coat on the ground, grabbed it and left. Yeg ran after them to retrieve his coat; Talbert struck Yeg in the face, and Weston fatally stabbed him with a knife. Talbert tried to escape but was pursued and captured by Napa police after violently resisting arrest. When asked why he had attacked the man, Talbert complained that "the people were hiring Chinese while white men have to walk the roads."[283] Weston escaped and made his way to Salt Lake City, Utah, but was detained there on the murder charge and brought back to Napa to stand trial.

The case drew widespread attention throughout Napa, and the trial had to be moved to a larger courtroom to accommodate the crowds.[284] At his trial for murder, the Chinese witnesses had to speak through an interpreter. Weston continued to deny the murder, despite his knife being the one that killed Yeg Chum and the fact that he fled to Salt Lake City immediately after the crime. During deliberations, the jury initially polled seven to five in favor of acquittal, then eleven to one in favor, then finally all twelve men agreed to let Charles Weston go free.[285] This verdict was reached despite fourteen witnesses to the crime (all Chinese) and the accused escaping all the way to Utah to avoid trial. The only thing tilting the case in the white transient's favor was his race and the race of his victim. But it was enough.

There are common themes that run through much of the reporting about crimes committed against Chinese residents. Law enforcement responded to crimes quickly enough, but in many cases, if the victim were Chinese, there was not much of an attempt to capture the perpetrator if he was not apprehended on the spot. The Yeg Chum killing is an exception to that rule, in that the police went all the way to Salt Lake City to bring the accused back to Napa. It may have been due to the intense publicity surrounding the case. Another common theme is that punishments for similar crimes were not the same based on the race of the accused. Goy, a Chinese man who attacked a white man, needed to raise $500 just for bail money versus a penalty of just $30 for the Chinese man who assaulted a fellow Chinese earlier. And once the criminal was brought into the justice system, it was practically impossible for a Chinese victim to get a fair hearing requiring the agreement of a jury of twelve white men.[286] By the end of the nineteenth century, Chinese people could testify in court, but they still could not serve on juries. But just testifying in court could not guarantee that they would be given the same credibility as testimony from a white defendant or witness. Finally, the reporting of the crimes was different depending on the racial makeup of the attacker and victim. In many cases, the names of the Chinese people involved in the crimes were omitted, and it was just "a Chinaman."

Chapter 7

NAPA VALLEY ANTI-CHINESE MOVEMENTS

P rior to 1885, opposition to Chinese residents of the Napa Valley was intense but relatively unorganized. Explicit "Anti-Coolie" leagues, as they were called, did not form in St. Helena until 1885 and in Napa until 1886. The formal California anti-Chinese movement was only sporadically effective but always very vocal and persistent. It provided a foundation for local groups to form in the mid-1880s, although local organizations were relatively short-lived; Napa Valley's organizations were no exception.

Early opposition to Chinese immigration in California was spearheaded by labor groups that saw the expanding pool of cheap Chinese labor as a tool of large capital-intensive companies like steamships and railroads.[287] California had, by a wide margin, the largest population of Chinese immigrants of any state in the United States, and anti-Chinese forces from California were the most vocal and intense in the country.

TABLE 3. CHINESE POPULATION IN CALIFORNIA RELATIVE TO THE UNITED STATES[288]

	1870	*1880*	*1890*	*1900*
Chinese in United States	63,199	105,465	107,480	89,863
Chinese in California	49,277	75,132	72,472	45,753
Percentage in California	78%	71%	67%	51%

Until 1900, California contained more residents from China than all other states combined.

Statewide, opposition to Chinese immigrants from 1860 onward focused on economic competition of Chinese labor versus white labor, "immoral" practices like opium smoking and gambling and their unwillingness to assimilate to the Anglo-American culture of California.[289] These objections were very similar to the local objections of Napa Valley townspeople. The difference at the statewide level was the unique position of labor in the 1860s through 1880s California political landscape. California labor groups—such as the Workingman's Party of California, the State Federation of Labor and the Knights of Labor—were some of the few statewide interest groups that were tightly organized and focused largely on a single topic: opposition to Chinese immigration. California's political parties were roughly equal in strength, and no party was able to elect its candidate to governor more than twice in succession, often by very slim margins. Thus, the organized labor groups, though relatively small in membership, held enormous power in the state as each party took on more and more extreme "anti-Chinese" positions to win the labor vote, regardless of how intensely they personally felt about California's Chinese population. It was virtually impossible to win statewide without labor's endorsement.[290]

Many statewide anti-Chinese laws and taxes, implemented by politicians in the pocket of labor, were thrown out as unconstitutional by the courts. Anti-Chinese labor groups, led by Dennis Kearney and the Workingman's Party, decided to take a different approach and were instrumental in the construction and passage of the 1879 California Constitution, which had an entire article dedicated to the prohibition of Chinese employment in California. Among the provisions in Article XIX, titled simply "Chinese," were:

SEC. 2. No corporation now existing or hereafter formed under the laws of this State, shall, after the adoption of this Constitution, employ directly or indirectly, in any capacity, any Chinese or Mongolian. The Legislature shall pass such laws as may be necessary to enforce this provision.

SEC. 3. No Chinese shall be employed on any State, county, municipal, or other public work, except in punishment for crime.

SEC. 4. The presence of foreigners ineligible to become citizens of the United States is declared to be dangerous to the well-being of the State, and the Legislature shall discourage their immigration by all the means within its power.

As with other statewide measures, Article XIX was declared unconstitutional a year later based on the court challenge by Napa Valley's Sulphur Bank Mine. California politicians then turned to the national political stage and were instrumental in gaining the passage of the Federal 1882 Chinese Exclusion Act, which effectively forbade further immigration by Chinese laborers.

California labor organizations began to lose power and status beginning in 1880.[291] Anti-Chinese agitation at the state level was largely unorganized during the first part of the 1880s. In February 1886, the California Non-Partisan Anti-Chinese Association was created during a statewide anti-Chinese convention in San Jose, California. C.F. McGlashan of Truckee was elected chairman of the organization, and Reverend N.F. Ravlin was chosen as state organizer.[292] One month later, another statewide convention was held in Sacramento during which a resolution was passed, amid great debate, to employ a boycott against local businesses or people who employed Chinese employees.[293] McGlashan and Ravlin would be frequent visitors to the Napa Valley throughout 1886, speaking at local anti-Chinese clubs and helping to educate and rally the local population to get rid of its Chinese inhabitants.

St. Helena

The first formal "Anti-Chinese League" in the Napa Valley was formed in St. Helena on November 27, 1885. An estimated three hundred to four hundred "tax-payers" attended the first regularly scheduled meeting on November 30. The core committee organizing the league included John Mavity, a real estate broker and director of the local Seventh-day Adventist Church; Phil O'Donnell, owner of the largest dry goods store in town; John Marquette, a leader of the United Workmen Lodge; E. Heymann, owner of the Railroad House, a local bar and billiard hall, as well as a vineyard owner; George Osborn, trustee of the Workingmen's club, vineyard owner and farmer; Charles Howard, town trustee and farmer; and F. Sciaroni, vineyard owner and owner of a dance and dining hall. These men were some of the leading merchants and politically connected citizens in town.[294]

The arguments against Chinese immigrants fell into the familiar patterns used by the statewide anti-Chinese leagues organized by labor groups: the presence of Chinese residents led to moral degradation of the youth and unfair labor competition, and they were unable or unwilling to assimilate. The group passed the following resolution at the first meeting:

WHEREAS, It is common knowledge that the existence among us of Chinese denizens tends to corrupt the youth of our community, by forcing them into competition with a degraded race, or into idleness, and by bringing them into familiar contact with scenes and habits of unthrift, filth and vice, and by giving force to the vicious conviction that labor such as Chinese may perform is degrading to our youth and populace; and

WHEREAS, It is true that the employment of Chinese in this vicinity is preventing many of our people from obtaining labor at once honorable and necessary for the moral and physical support and growth of themselves and their families; and

WHEREAS, It appears that the Chinese are becoming more numerous in our midst and probably in our state, and that they are by practicing religion opposed to our habits and customs, into our National and State laws, and local ordinances, and refuse to adopt or be governed by them, either in trade, in policy of action, or in that common cleanliness which materially avoids and prevents the spread of disease, and makes habitation tolerable; therefore

Resolved, *That we proceed to organize a protective Anti-Chinese League.*

That the chief objective of such League shall be to effect the entire exclusion of the Chinese from the corporate limits of St. Helena and its vicinity by any and every *lawful means.*

That in furtherance of said object the Secretary of this meeting shall immediately receive the signature of all persons desirous of pledging themselves to support the object of said League, and that at a subsequent meeting of the persons so pledging themselves a permanent organization of said league shall be effected.

In St. Helena, 160 citizens signed this resolution. The *St. Helena Star* newspaper, frequently a critic of the Chinese residents in town, applauded the formation of the league. It specifically called out the local Chinatown, "with its filthy and diseased heathens, its dens of infamy, and its reeking cesspools," which was the first thing visitors to town saw when they arrived from the south when traveling up valley.

The *Star* did provide a notable caveat to its endorsement of the league. While it wholeheartedly agreed with tearing down Chinatown, it worried that if it convinced Chinese laborers to leave the Napa Valley, "it would be impossible to get help at the proper time to gather and care for the grape crop." Once a suitable replacement labor force was found for the Chinese worker, then the paper would agree with the sentiment that "the Chinese must go."[295]

On Saturday, January 30, 1886, flyers went up throughout St. Helena announcing a gathering the following Monday at the town hall, where the townspeople would determine the best way to expel the Chinese residents from town. Monday's meeting was well attended, and everyone agreed that members of the St. Helena Anti-Chinese League should meet the very next day to begin the expulsion. By 4:00 p.m. on Tuesday, a group of two to three hundred members of the Anti-Chinese League had met in front of the town hall to the ringing of bells and the blowing of whistles. They were formed into a line by W.T. Simmons, a justice of the peace and a leading Republican Party man, who cautioned the crowd to be orderly. They lined up and marched to Chinatown accompanied by a militaristic drum cadence to demand that all Chinese residents leave town within ten days. Chinatown residents heard the commotion, boarded up all the doors and windows and refused to come out and meet the mob. The police were present and persuaded a few of the Chinese merchants to come out to at least hear the demands of the crowd. Once the message was delivered that the Chinese had to leave, the mostly peaceful crowd dispersed.[296]

Given this highly charged and potentially dangerous environment, it is unsurprising that it was during this year, 1886, that Jue Joe decided to leave St. Helena and his vineyard labor job behind and take a job with the Southern Pacific Railroad that took him, eventually, to Southern California. Other than Jue Joe's exodus, we don't know how many Chinese laborers decided to leave St. Helena or the Napa Valley based on this outpouring of discrimination and hate from the townspeople, but it is likely that quite a few, if they had the means and weren't tied to the community, may have decided it was time to leave.

Although it may have seemed like everyone in town marched to Chinatown to demand the Chinese leave, the townspeople of St. Helena were not unified in their desire to immediately drive out the Chinese residents. In fact, it was a surprise to many of the influential and wealthy land owners in town. Later that week on Saturday, February 6, many vineyard owners and wine merchants met at the Turner Hall in downtown St. Helena to discuss the anti-Chinese group's demand that the Chinese depart. They were worried about the labor needed to harvest their vineyards and the legality of the crowd's actions on February 2. They rejected the violent overtones of the anti-Chinese group and their demands that the Chinese immediately leave.[297]

One of the vineyard owners said that they were willing "to replace the Chinamen with white labor as fast as possible, but we cannot afford to allow our interests to suffer as they necessarily will if the Chinese are forced to leave before reliable white labor can be secured." He went on: "There is another reason why we object to the course being pursued by the anti-Chinese organization and that is, their acts are unlawful. Our people have no right to force the Chinamen to pick up and leave their property, and thus cause them serious pecuniary loss." The vineyard owners, a very powerful and influential group in town, were worried that if the anti-Chinese group ended up getting violent with the Chinese and forcibly evicted them, the town of St. Helena—and by extension the wealthier taxpayers—would eventually have to pay damages and reparations.

The argument between the two sides got heated and almost came to blows. The pastor of the Presbyterian church in town, Reverend James Mitchell, addressed both sides of the debate when the discussion threatened to turn violent. He said that he "was glad to see the two interests, capital and labor, represented in this meeting," and he called for a peaceful resolution. He called on businesses, the vineyard owners and wine merchants to reach out to labor to see if there was a solution. He also called on labor not to resort to violence to get its way. Both sides seemed mollified by Mitchell's remarks, and the meeting soon broke up peacefully.[298]

The split between labor and capital on how to handle their "Chinese problem" did not get resolved. Despite the governance of leading citizens in town and the large crowds at the initial meetings, the St. Helena Anti-Chinese League appears to have had a short life and produced few tangible results beyond its initial resolution and the march on Chinatown. It could not find a way to expel the Chinese from town without resorting to intimidation and violence. Powerful land owners could not be without the Chinese labor that was so critical to the success of the agricultural interests of St. Helena. Napa's Anti-Chinese League, on the other hand, was more united, much longer lived and took more decisive actions.

NAPA

By many measures, the city of Napa was more accepting of its Chinese population than St. Helena. Chinatown was adjacent to downtown Napa and did not seem to provoke much agitation or outrage among its citizens. Many white Napa residents visited and shopped in Chinatown, which happened seldom, if at all, in St. Helena, outside of its gambling halls and opium dens. Chinese residents of Napa were spread around several different sections of the city, and central Napa was much more integrated than St. Helena. While the main newspaper in town, the *Napa Register*, had plenty of negative things to say about Napa's Chinese residents, it rarely adopted the vitriolic language and attitudes of the *St. Helena Star*. Napa's Anti-Chinese League, on the other hand, formed just two months after St. Helena's, was much more organized and effective. From the beginning, it had a plan, based on a coordinated boycott, for ridding the Chinese from the city.

Napa's Anti-Chinese League was formed on February 11, 1886, in the downtown opera house to an "overflowing" crowd. Like the St. Helena organization, it was founded by leading citizens of the town, including Chairman F.L. Jackson, who worked in real estate and insurance; President H.C. Gesford, Esq., a lawyer in town and member of the board of education; and G.M. Francis, who was active in Republican state politics. Unlike the St. Helena organization, which advocated for a swift, yet lawful, expulsion of the Chinese from town without providing specifics, the Napa Anti-Chinese League provided a very precise action plan right from its first meeting:

> *Resolved, That we, the people at Napa, in public meeting assembled, deprecate all violence or commands emanating from any source that may result in violence.*
>
> *Resolved, That we urge Congress, with all the emphasis words can convey, to pass such laws as shall effectually do away with the present return certification system, by which Chinaman may either return or gain unlawful entry into this country.*
>
> *Resolved, That we hereby pledge ourselves, at the earliest possible period, to desist from employing Chinese labor in any capacity whatsoever, or purchasing goods manufactured or produced by Chinese in this country.*
>
> *Resolved, That our City Trustees be requested to look into the sanitary conditions of the Chinese quarters and then pass and strictly enforce such ordinances as are necessary to make the Chinaman live like white people and observe the white man's laws of health.*
>
> *Resolved, That our police officers be required to act more vigilantly in suppressing opium dens and Chinese gambling games.*
>
> *Resolved, that we hereby organize ourselves into an association to be known as the "Anti-Chinese League of the City of Napa," having for its object the ends set forth in the foregoing resolutions.*

The Napa Anti-Chinese League also integrated itself into a broader movement by electing a slate to represent Napa County at the statewide Anti-Chinese Convention being held in Sacramento the following month. W.T. Simmons, the man who led the St. Helena mob through downtown to confront the Chinese in Chinatown, was one of the members of the slate.[299] The announcement of a statewide Anti-Chinese Convention was first reported by local papers on January 29, 1886, and may have been the impetus for the formation of Napa's group so it could be formally represented.[300]

The organizational acumen of Napa's Anti-Chinese League was immediately apparent. It created an Executive Committee to drive the agenda of subsequent meetings, an Enrollment Committee to support recruiting new members to the group, a committee to find a permanent meeting place, a committee on Chinese vegetable peddlers and a committee to address the one business area that the Chinese business owners continually out-competed white business owners: the laundry.

On March 6, 1886, the Committee on Steam Laundry formed a joint stock company with the purpose of establishing a white-owned laundry in Napa. The committee decided that providing a "good steam laundry in Napa where washing can be done at reasonable prices, will prove a more effective way of getting rid of the Chinese than black-listing people to refuse to join the league."[301] Within one week, it had secured subscriptions to half of the initial public offering. Remarkably, it had to turn down existing shareholders who wanted to buy more shares in order to allow more people to participate in the venture.[302] This approach of trying to entice customers away from Chinese-owned businesses with a competing venture was a considerably different approach than that of the St. Helena group to march to Chinatown and demand they leave within ten days.

The Enrollment Committee created a pledge based on the original set of resolutions put forth by the Anti-Chinese League that prospective members must sign to become supporters:

> *We, the undersigned citizens of Napa County hereby organize ourselves into an association to be known as the "Anti-Chinese League of the City of Napa" having for its object the expulsion of the Chinese from our midst, and we hereby pledge ourselves to vigorously adopt all legal, peaceable methods to secure that end.*
>
> *We and each of us further pledge ourselves at the earliest possible period to be determined by this League to desist from employing Chinese labor in*

any capacity whatsoever, or purchasing goods manufactured or produced by Chinese labor in America, and renting lands or houses to them.[303]

The league adopted the pledge and instructed members of the committee to go around the city and recruit people by having them sign the pledge. Within one week, the committee had four hundred names on the list.[304] There was debate about whether the names of men who refused to sign the pledge should be read aloud at subsequent meetings. The *Napa County Reporter* and the *Napa Register* both editorialized that this would be a bad idea. While the *Reporter* agreed with the aims of the Anti-Chinese League, it said that publicly shaming men who did not sign would "needlessly antagonize all those who do not believe just as they do." It also was concerned that judges and other public officials who ostensibly are supposed to be impartial should not sign the list. "What good therefore," the editorial continued, "can come from reading of a black list? In this fight against the Chinamen the white people should be as united as possible."[305]

The pledge to avoid purchasing items manufactured by Chinese labor proved difficult for some local businessmen. Frank Wright, who sold boots and shoes in Napa, said that he fully supported the goals of the Anti-Chinese League, but he could not find any slippers manufactured anywhere on the West Coast that were not produced by Chinese labor. He asked the league if he would be in violation of his pledge if he went ahead and stocked Chinese-made slippers in his store. After some discussion, the Executive Committee decreed that if there was not a white labor alternative, then he was allowed to purchase Chinese slippers this one time only for display, but if he persisted in stocking Chinese goods in his store, "he would do so at his peril."[306]

Discussions of whether to shun businesses that sold Chinese goods or used Chinese labor was a hot topic of conversation. "Do you favor boycotting?" was a familiar question around town. The *Napa Register* was worried about what an organized boycott of specific Napa businesses would do to the economic health of the city. It tried to walk a fine line saying that individuals had a right to buy from whatever business they wanted,

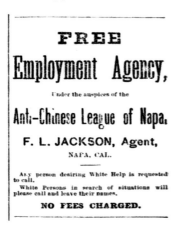

FREE
Employment Agency,

Under the auspices of the

Anti-Chinese League of Napa,

F. L. JACKSON, Agent,

NAPA, CAL.

Any person desiring White Help is requested to call.

White Persons in search of situations will please call and leave their names.

NO FEES CHARGED.

The Anti-Chinese League opened an employment office for white laborers. *From the* Napa County Reporter, *April 2, 1886.*

but a group action that coordinated a boycott and shamed people into not patronizing certain businesses would be unfair to the business community and could escalate quickly. It worried that a simple boycott "which means the withdrawal of all patronage from the Chinese and when people voluntarily pledge themselves to do this thing they are taking a long stride toward a better era in the history of our State." But it worried that a boycott could spin out of control and could take "for its badge the skull and cross bones, law and order ends and violence begins."

Furthermore, the *Register* charged that the statewide coordinators of such boycotts, like Reverend N.F. Ravlin, who made $150 per month, were touting slogans like people should boycott "until the employers of Chinese do one of two things—discharge their Mongolians or die." They reprinted a letter that a business owner in Marysville, near Sacramento, received because of a local boycott there:

> *Get rid of your Chiney help as quick as possible being a true friend of yours I do not which to see you come to Some untimely end all on account of a cussid mongolian whom you can replace with a few cts more by white Labor.*

The *Register* implored the Napa townspeople to patronize white-owned laundries, not buy from Chinese vegetable peddlers and employ white labor whenever possible. But it cautioned against boycotting any local businesses just because someone told them to.[307]

The league eventually decided to make boycotting Chinese goods a central tenet of the organization. On April 17, 1886, the league passed a resolution requiring "that members of the League hereafter refuse to patronize all Chinese goods."[308] Some were worried about the practical effects of such a boycott. The *Napa Register* wrote an editorial a week later cautioning the league:

> *They will say to the people: "You must not sell to or deal with Chinamen, their patrons, or employers." How many members of the Napa Anti-Chinese League are ready to put such preaching into practice? How many of them still patronize Chinese laundries? And with what consistency can those who do ask fruit men and manufacturers to discharge their Chinamen? If the man whose name is on the League roll still patronizes the Chinese laundryman because he cannot afford to pay white persons 50 to 200 per cent more for the same work, why should he not accord the*

same method of reasoning to his neighbor who has land to till and crops to save as well as soiled linen to cleanse? Consistency is a charming thing to have and we commend it to all boycotters who still have their washing down by Ah Sing.[309]

The following month, the league, in a meeting attended by about two hundred people, decided to ratchet up the intensity of the boycott.[310] In addition to not purchasing goods made or produced by Chinese labor, it voted to "boycott all persons employing or in any manner patronizing Chinamen." It debated further whether to publish the names of all people being boycotted for this transgression in the local newspapers so they could be blacklisted by the broader community. The *Napa Weekly Journal* newspaper joined the *Napa Register* in advocating against this course of action. The *Journal* made no secret that it wished to be rid of the "Chinese curse." But it viewed the aggressive boycotting and blacklisting as a "two-edged sword" that would create bitter animosity among townspeople toward one another, destroy businesses and cause a series of reciprocal boycotts that would eventually lead to distrust and lawsuits. It would undo the "good work" that had been done by the Napa League, including driving Chinese laborers from the tannery and the woolen mills.[311]

The *Napa County Reporter* joined in the debate and said that it would refuse to publish any blacklisted names in its paper. The *Napa Register*, whose editor was one of the founders of the Anti-Chinese League, said that it disagreed with the idea of publishing blacklisted names but said it would do it if the league took out a paid-for advertisement in the paper.[312] In fact, the *Register* proclaimed that it would "publish as an advertisement and at reduced rates, the names to be boycotted, if a faithful list of the boycotters [i.e., those members of the league who favored such action] is presented for publication at the same time. We need both lists in order to make a fair and complete showing. How could we be more generous than that?"[313]

While the initial reporting and the debate among the papers treated the publication of the blacklist as unanimously agreed to by the league, the league started backpedaling almost immediately. Despite personal accounts of the passage of the blacklist proposal at the meeting, it began to be positioned as something that was discussed but not passed. It is impossible to know if this is true, or if the league was surprised by the vehement objections to the publication of the blacklisted names and tried to rewrite its position. Gesford, the president of the league, put out a statement that only the boycott itself was in effect, not publishing of the names of those to be boycotted.

Those names, however, would still be read aloud at league meetings.[314] This distinction seems to be somewhat of a compromise, since presumably any of the hundreds of people who had been attending the meetings could have spread the word about which companies should be avoided. But if the whole goal of the boycott and blacklist was to drive business down for transgressing businesses, it is hard to imagine why the league wouldn't want to try to publicly shame the offenders.

On June 12, 1886, Reverend N.F. Ravlin, who coordinated Anti-Chinese Leagues at the state level, spoke to "a large audience" at a meeting of the Napa League. While his speech was both "conservative" and "strongly anti-Chinese," he said that a boycott should only be used as a last resort.[315] He cautioned the group about instituting boycotts of businesses that employed Chinese labor unless and until sufficient white labor was available. Only if stable, hardworking white labor was available and a business refused to fire its Chinese employees to hire the white laborer should it be boycotted. The business did not have to hire "unreliable, drunken white laborers" if that was all that was available.

Notably, three weeks after the league's boycott resolution was introduced, no one had turned in a single business for employing Chinese labor unnecessarily.[316] The idea of a boycott, so enthusiastically pursued and debated through the spring and summer, never materialized into anything substantial. The *San Francisco Examiner* in November 1886 reported that the statewide anti-Chinese boycott was "now in effect dead."[317] The pushback of most newspapers in town, the reluctance of many townspeople to turn against local businesses and the lack of available replacement labor made a boycott impractical for many. Once the boycott idea failed, public activities of the Napa Anti-Chinese League seemed to wither away as well.

YOUNTVILLE

The small town of Yountville, eight miles north of Napa, did not have a significant Chinese population, but it had its own anti-Chinese group, at least for a single meeting. Nearly 250 people gathered in McGillis Hall in Yountville on February 19, 1886, to "express their views and take action in the matter of Chinese immigration." Unlike organizations in St. Helena and Napa, which were led by businessmen, the Yountville group was led by its district attorney, Mr. Hogan, who spoke for almost an hour. His speech was followed by H.C. Gesford of the Napa Anti-Chinese League, who provided an update on the events in Napa. Both Hogan and Gesford expressed strong anti-Chinese sentiment but cautioned the assembled group to be lawful and careful.[318] The group did not have any subsequent meetings and likely was absorbed into the St. Helena or Napa groups, which were in larger towns and were better organized.

CALISTOGA

The Panic of 1893 spurred a nationwide depression that resulted in the closure of thousands of businesses and farms. Perhaps because of those severe economic pressures, Calistoga's formal anti-Chinese movement was organized around securing jobs for white farm laborers. In August 1893, an organization named the White Labor Union was founded in Calistoga by fifty-seven Calistoga residents. In their organizing resolution, they demanded that "none but white labor be employed in the present fruit harvest; and therefore request all employers of labor, to give resident white labor preference above Japanese, Chinese, or other outside labor."[319]

Later that year, they claimed they found jobs for 110 white laborers around Calistoga. They also took credit for forcing Mr. W.B. Bourn, who owned Greystone, the largest wine storage facility in the world just north of St. Helena, to terminate 80 Chinese labors and replace them with white laborers.[320] Perhaps coincidentally, Bourn sold the wine storage facility six months later.[321] After 1893, there is no record of any activity of the White Labor Union. The union may have felt its job was completed or increasingly unnecessary, especially as the population of Chinese workers dropped precipitously in the late 1890s.

OPPOSING THE ANTI-CHINESE MOVEMENT

Very few local people or organizations publicly opposed the anti-Chinese movements that were prevalent during the 1880s and 1890s. The Chinese Six Companies out of San Francisco provided legal assistance to fight specific instances of discrimination, as it did in the first Sam Kee laundry case, but it had limited direct influence in the Napa Valley.

Occasionally, there were reports of specific people challenging anti-Chinese statutes, like Reverend Richard Wylie, who spoke from the pulpit in defense of specific laws unfairly targeting Chinese businessmen like Sam

Kee in the community. More frequent were the silent protests against anti-Chinese policies, like when no member of the Napa Anti-Chinese League referred a single business to be boycotted after weeks and months of threats, even though clearly many businesses were still employing Chinese labor. There were also the many citizens who would shop in Chinese stores, take their laundry to Chinese laundries and hire Chinese laborers to do work around their homes and farms. These people never publicly announced their positive (or at least neutral) position on the "Chinese question," likely because it would have served no purpose except to call attention to themselves. They did, however, express their opinions with their pocketbooks, where they shopped and who they hired.

The one group that did formally, publicly and repeatedly stand up against the worst aspects of anti-Chinese sentiment were, unsurprisingly, the leading employers of Chinese workers in towns—the vineyard owners, farmers and other business owners. In St. Helena, they collectively put a stop to the attempted forced expulsion of Chinese residents from Chinatown. In Napa, they argued forcefully against boycotting businesses that employed Chinese labor. Leonard Coates, the owner of Napa Valley Nurseries, wrote an impassioned public letter in the heat of the anti-Chinese movements in the *Napa Register* in 1886 asking to represent "the 'other side' on this Anti-Chinese agitation."[322]

The *Register* printed the letter on the front page to ensure that everyone had a chance to read his opinion. His letter started with the standard disclaimers that his "side" was not necessarily in favor of Chinese immigration or opposed to the federal Chinese restriction laws. He did assert that as fruit growers, grape growers and other businessmen, they had a right to run their businesses, which required a large capital investment, as efficiently as they are able. Surprisingly, he did not stress that the Chinese workers were the best low-cost labor option; rather, he emphasized the unique skills that the Chinese agricultural workers brought to the business that made them the best choice period:

> *The farmer in California has for years depended very largely upon Chinese laborers to pick and pack his fruit, to dry the fruit, prepare it for the cannery, gather the grapes for the wine maker, make raisins, do the budding, grafting, pruning, and almost all the routine of work, skilled and unskilled of the horticulturist. As a result we have now a large force of competent, skilled laborer, who have been patiently instructed in their business for the last 15 or 20 years and longer.*

He also challenged the racial element of the anti-Chinese leagues in very plain language:

> *Would these same citizens dare—we use the term advisedly—to intimidate or persecute foreigners from any European country who may be here? Then why this unreasoning, unmanly, unjust crusade against the Chinese? Attack your legislators, your government, if you will, for opening the Golden Gate to these people, for offering inducements to come, for receiving them kindly and giving them constant employment.* The law *will prevent you from doing any harm to such. Where, we say, is the right, or the justice in resorting to intimidation, persecution, or "boycotting"?*

He closed his letter by reasserting the rights of the businesses to conduct business the best way they could. The terminology and tone are certainly paternalistic and focused on their businesses, not the well-being of the Chinese laborer, but in this case, they were both parts of the same solution:

> *We recognize no right by which you dictate to us what we shall do; we recognize no right by which you shall seek to intimidate our laborers into leaving us, thus ruining our crops; we will protect our properties, our laborers, ourselves. Time alone can work this change; it cannot be done in one or in two years, without enormous sacrifice and ruination, and without infringing upon the rights of the individual, and incurring a lasting shame, not only upon this State, but upon the whole country.*[323]

We cannot know how many people shared his view, but we do know that the boycott he opposed ended up a dismal failure.

DIFFERING APPROACHES, SAME RESULT

St. Helena and Napa Anti-Chinese Leagues followed very different paths to try to push Chinese residents out of their towns. The St. Helena League was formed first, before any of the guiding principles were set forth by the state-level conventions. Many St. Helena townspeople were blinded with their hatred of the Chinatown on their southern border. As soon as a large group of vocal anti-Chinese citizens got together, they could not help themselves but to march down to Chinatown to terrorize the Chinese residents. They did not account for the economic and political clout of the vineyard and land owning class who needed the Chinese workers to make their enterprises successful. Their formal Anti-Chinese League, although it attracted hundreds to its first few meetings, dissolved almost immediately in the face of opposition by the wealthier citizens in town.

The Napa League followed the model put forth at the statewide anti-Chinese convention, but the result was not much different. It took an organized, prudent and legalistic approach that prioritized the boycotting of local businesses that employed Chinese labor as the convention had directed. It ran into unexpected resistance from most of the local papers when the exercise of a boycott was extrapolated to its logical conclusion. Eventually, the Napa organization ran into the same issue the St. Helena organization did—there just was no substitute for Chinese labor for most businesses that employed them. However, both leagues were just a bit too early, given demographic changes brought on by the eventual result of the 1882 Chinese Exclusion Act and the arrival of an acceptable alternative labor force: the Italians.

It is worth noting that anti-Chinese sentiment and actions in the Napa Valley were less violent than in other parts of the West at this time. In 1885, two notorious episodes of anti-Chinese violence and intimidation occurred north of Napa. The Chinatown in Tacoma, Washington, was burned to the ground by angry townspeople, and many were forced to flee south to Portland, Oregon, or north to Canada. Hundreds of Chinese workers in the Northern California town of Eureka were forcibly marched out of town amid threats of being hanged in what became known as the "Eureka Roundup."[324] Despite angry rhetoric, the relationship of Chinese workers in the Napa Valley, especially in the town of Napa, was mostly focused on economic pressure.

CONCLUSION

The Chinese population in the late nineteenth and early twentieth centuries peaked in the early 1880s and then began a slow downward trend through 1900, 1910 and 1920. There are two main factors that contribute to the decline. First, Chinese labor immigration into the United States dropped dramatically after the passage of the 1882 Chinese Exclusion Act and the subsequent passage of the Geary Act in 1892. The decline was aggravated by the lack of families or children of Chinese workers in the Napa Valley. Second, the need for Chinese labor, especially in the vineyard and agricultural areas, diminished greatly due to a slump in demand for wine, technological innovations and the introduction of a replacement labor class, Italian immigrants. The peak of anti-Chinese sentiment coincided with the peak of Chinese population around the 1880s. It was likely the slow but inexorable population decline of the Chinese in the late 1880s and 1890s that reduced the intensity of anti-Chinese activism.

TABLE 4. CHINESE AND ITALIAN POPULATION IN NAPA COUNTY, 1870–1920.[325]

	1870	1880	1890	1900	1910	1920
White	6,725	12,160	15,426	15,857	14,154	15,930
Chinese	263	907	875	541	205	126
Italian	25	71	320	401	1,017	1,084
Total	**7,163**	**13,235**	**16,411**	**16,451**	**19,800**	**20,678**

There was a significant decline in the Chinese population at the same time the Italian population was growing between 1890 and 1910. The population of Italian and Chinese residents of Napa County was roughly equal somewhere around 1902.

CHINESE EXCLUSION ACTS AND THE DWINDLING CHINESE POPULATION

The *St. Helena Star* called for August 4, 1882, to be made a holiday because it was the day that the 1882 Chinese Exclusion Act would officially go into effect.[326] Despite the wishes of the *Star*, the Chinese population were not immediately excluded or removed from St. Helena. The 1882 Exclusion Act barred additional immigration for ten years by Chinese laborers from China and declared that no Chinese person was eligible for U.S. citizenship. The act was the first federal law to bar immigration of a particular racial group into the United States. It had the unintended side effect of dramatically increasing Chinese immigration in the early 1880s. Since the act was several years in the making, any Chinese laborer who was considering immigrating to America knew that they had to make the decision to go before the law took effect. Consequently, there was a significant increase in immigration from China in the years leading up to 1882. The year 1882 saw the immigration of almost 40,000 Chinese into the United States, almost twice the number of any previous year. There were loopholes, like whether a Chinese laborer could immigrate to America from a country other than China, that allowed another 8,000 immigrants in 1883. That loophole was closed in 1884, when there were just 279 Chinese immigrants into the United States. The restriction on Chinese immigration was further strengthened by an 1888 law that tightened restrictions on the immigration of laborers for the next twenty years, and further laws were passed in 1892 and 1904 that effectively shut down all new immigration from China.[327] The 1892 Geary Act went far beyond just prohibiting immigration. It required Chinese residents or persons of Chinese descent to have their picture taken and apply for a certificate of residency to avoid arrest and deportation. It was still possible to emigrate from China, as Jue Joe did in 1906 when he reentered the United States as a returning successful merchant, but he could not have done so as a new immigrant laborer.

The impact of the Geary Act was far reaching. The Chinese Six Companies organized the largest civil disobedience movement among Chinese in America to oppose the act by not registering as required. It asked every Chinese to donate a dollar—more than a day's wages for many—to the legal fund needed to challenge the Geary Act. The attorneys hired by the Chinese Six Companies failed to win the case of *Fong Yue Ting v. U.S.*, which would have declared the Geary Act unconstitutional. It was a blow to the Chinese in the Napa Valley, in California and across the nation and a humiliating defeat for the Six Companies. There was mourning in all Chinatowns from San Francisco to New York.

In 1887, the Chinese workers experienced the peak of their economic power, as demonstrated by their successful strikes for more wages working both in the vineyards and hop yards. By 1890, the demographic realities were too significant to ignore. The vast majority of Chinese in the Napa Valley were single men. While there were some marriages and some families, the number of Chinese children in the Valley prior to 1900 never exceeded twenty-five (see Table 7 in the appendix), and those numbers could not replace Chinese laborers who either returned to China, left the Napa Valley for safer environments in places like San Francisco or died due to illness, old age, workplace injury or violence.

There was more flexibility and longevity in the urban areas. Some of Napa's Chinese families still made a living in Chinatown and surrounding areas for years after 1900. Yip Fong, who was born in Napa in 1919 and was raised in Chinatown, remembered Chinese men visiting the temple when she was a little girl, although by that time the population of Chinatown had dwindled to about thirty-five. Fong, granddaughter of Chan Wah Jack, lived with her parents and her uncles in the back of Wah Jack's Lai Hing Company.[328] Yet by 1930, there were only seventeen people living in Chinatown—and ten of them were part of Fong's family. They were all moved out of Chinatown in April 1930 at the city's expense to clean up the polluted Napa River and eventually make way for a yacht harbor that was never built.[329]

THE ARRIVAL OF THE ITALIANS

The *Napa Register* was very enthusiastic about the possibility that Italian immigrants could replace Chinese workers as early as 1880:

A LARGE NUMBER OF ITALIANS find employment in the vineyards in town and vicinity. Chinamen need never apply—that is hardly ever—at this very busy season of the year. Although they quickly learn to do most every kind of work, they cannot be made to understand the philosophy of pruning. "I have never yet seen a Chinaman who could prune," said a grape grower of large experience.

As for the Italians they are a very industrious, sober and trustworthy class of workmen. Natives of a wine country, they are perfectly at home in vineyards and in the wine cellars.[330]

The *Napa Register* article may have been premature in thinking that Italian labor would rescue local vineyard owners from the "curse" of the low-paid, hardworking Chinese vineyard workers, but its overall prediction ultimately proved true. Italians were some of the earliest European immigrants into the Napa Valley, but they did not reach sufficient numbers to become a dominant labor class until 1890, about the time when the Chinese population started its rapid decline. Napa County's first Italian immigrant was Lorenzo Carbone in 1863 from Genoa, Italy.[331] In 1867, Lorenzo and his brothers Nicola and Antonio Carbone established the first Italian produce garden on Coombsville Road. This may have been the same field where Yeg Chum was murdered during 1894.

The Napa Valley wine industry followed global wine trends and went into a decline in the 1890s due to several factors. Demand for wine slowly declined starting in the late 1880s due to the early phases of the anti-alcohol Prohibition movement, which would eventually culminate in the passage of the Eighteenth Amendment in 1919. An 1890 California report on the state's viticulture industry stated that overall wine production had not increased since 1887, and there was no "reason to anticipate any great increase within the next three or four years." Consequently, prices for wine grapes were also at an all-time low due to lack of demand.

At the same time, the Phylloxera insect blight that had so affected France in the 1870s and had provided an opening for Napa Valley wines to gain worldwide recognition began to devastate local vineyards as well. Thousands of acres were affected, and the only solution in much of the Napa Valley was to graft older, disease-resistant vines onto existing plants—a time-consuming and expensive proposition.[332] E.C. Priber, the viticultural commissioner for the Napa District, published a report in August 1890 that outlined the extent of the problem: "Only about 10 per cent of the fifteen thousand acres are planted in resistant vines. The experience with resistant vines in France, where the production is now rapidly increasing, in consequence of the replanting of those vineyards which were destroyed by the Phylloxera, should teach us a lesson."[333]

The combination of falling demand, the Phylloxera plague and an economic depression in 1893 caused many businesses and banks to fold. This meant that many wineries and vineyards were sold or abandoned. Many of the Italian immigrant families, as the *Register* noted, were experienced with winemaking, as it was a popular occupation in Italy. Plenty of vineyard and winery owners sold their businesses to the incoming Italians, who were able to both run the businesses and work as field hands, negating the need for Chinese labor.[334] Thus the foundational mythos of Italian winemakers in Napa Valley began.

The constant lack of labor available to the vineyard owners, which caused Chinese labor to be in great demand and eventually allowed them to successfully strike for higher wages, eventually led vineyard owners to optimize their crops for fewer and fewer laborers. They planted vineyards in wide-enough rows to allow for the use of a wider plow that required fewer men and horses to till the soil. They took advantage of newer mechanized cultivation tools that required less manpower to operate. By 1900, a single laborer could tend a cultivated vineyard as large as twenty acres, with additional labor only required during the month-long harvest.[335]

Finally, the Phylloxera spread caused many vineyard owners to have to replant their vines. By that time, the Board of Viticultural Commissioners was recommending that vines be planted such that they could be harvested about three feet off the ground. This removed the dreaded "stoop labor" that had previously been required and made it more acceptable for Italian and other white laborers to work in the vineyards during harvest.[336]

The Forgotten Chinese

The Chinese contributions to the Napa Valley have been only sporadically acknowledged or celebrated. There are no monuments, plaques or any other physical recognition of the Chinese who lived, worked and died in Calistoga, St. Helena, Rutherford or Oakville. Napa has two plaques, a small parklet and a fountain mosaic that provide a modest commemoration of the Chinese contribution. On the other hand, it is noteworthy that the local historical societies in both Napa and St. Helena have done significant work spotlighting Chinese contributions through activities like historical reviews, lectures and cemetery tours.

Napa's Chinatown was razed in 1930. Almost fifty years later, E Clampus Vitus, an organization "dedicated to the study and preservation of the heritage of the American West," sponsored the installation of two plaques on Napa's First Street Bridge at a spot overlooking the former location of Chinatown.[337] One plaque described Chinatown itself, and the other honored Shuck Chan, son of Chan Wah Jack and "the sole surviving member of Napa's once-flourishing Chinatown business community." The city dedicated Sunday, August 19, 1979, as "Shuck Chan Day" in honor of the occasion.[338]

The Chinatown dedication plaque was oddly clinical in its description and not entirely correct. There were still Chinese people living in Chinatown in 1929, but the city moved them out in 1930 to make way for a flood-control project and a yacht harbor that never materialized. Notably absent in the dedication is the lack of any context of the contributions that Chinese citizens made to Napa or even the special place that Chinatown held for both Chinese and white townspeople during its heyday:

Chinatown

Napa's Chinatown was situated on both sides of First Street from this point west to Napa Creek. It occupied the area south of First to the Napa River where the Joss House stood near the juncture of Napa Creek off a narrow wagon road. East of the road were several wood framed houses on stilts and the Lai Hing Co. Additional Chinese houses and the Quong Shew Chong laundry were on the north side of First. The area was abandoned in 1929.

The plaque dedicated to Shuck Chan was slightly more enthusiastic but still was mostly a dry, factual representation:

Shuck Chan

To honor a leading citizen of Napa. He came here from China in 1989 at the age of three. The owner of Lai Hing Co. He and his wife Lee Kum were the last merchants of Chinatown.

There are local groups, like the Vallejo Napa Chinese Club, that have been pushing for improved signage and commemorations around the site of Napa's Chinatown for years. Their efforts may bear fruit in the future.

In 2017, Napa installed a parklet at the base of the First Street Bridge called "China Point Overlook" that consists of a large twelve-foot-tall sculpture called a moon gate. Unfortunately, the city ran short of funds during construction, so many elements were removed, including,

Left: The plaque commemorating Chinatown and Shuck Chen on Napa's First Street Bridge. *Author's collection.*

Below: Moon gate sculpture at China Point Overlook parklet. *Author's collection.*

presumably, any sort of description of what the sculpture or parklet might be commemorating.

Alan Shepp created a mosaic fountain in downtown Napa featuring vignettes of the Valley's role in the tale of the American West. He did include a section on a fire in Napa's Chinatown that destroyed many of the buildings. In 2014, the Chinese Cultural Heritage Foundation gave him an award for keeping that part of Napa's history alive.

THE UNIQUE IMPORTANCE OF THE CHINESE CONTRIBUTION

The Chinese contribution to the success of Napa Valley industry between 1870 and 1900 was felt across every major area of commerce in the region. Inexpensive Chinese labor was critical to the success of economic activities and roles such as viticulture, hop picking, tanneries, quicksilver mining, road and bridge construction, farm labor, store ownership, merchants, railroad maintenance, laundries, vegetable peddlers, waiters, domestic servants and cooks. The fact that Chinese workers were as successful as they were given the intense discrimination they faced socially, economically, legally and politically is nothing short of remarkable. They were simultaneously not allowed to be a part of the mainstream culture of the Napa Valley and disparaged for not assimilating to that culture.

For the most part, they were not allowed to live among the people for whom they worked and had to sleep and live in crowded ghettos and tenement housing. They were not allowed to bring their families to the United States to be with them. For the vast majority of the Chinese workers, there was no opportunity for a secure livelihood, marriage or having a family of their own.

They kept their cultural identity through traditions carried from their home country, worship in temples, eating familiar foods and through fraternal membership in organizations like the Chinese Free Masons, which operated as stand-ins for the families left behind. Their communities in various Chinatowns throughout the Napa Valley served as anchors to the culture they left back in China. They came to the United States to work hard and make money for their families back in China to have a better life.

They had to deal with a legal system that was both overtly and implicitly racist and refused, at almost every turn, to bring justice to aggrieved Chinese people or ensure that townspeople who attacked or murdered them served even a portion of their sentence. Yet the Chinese continued, despite their repeated losses in courts, to try to use the American legal system to receive justice. Sometimes they were successful, as they were able to remain in St. Helena's Chinatown for years despite overt attempts to overturn their leases. Yet every day they walked down the street of a town in the Napa Valley, they knew that they were viewed with suspicion by many of the people they saw and that if they were attacked, taken advantage of or simply discriminated against, there was very little they could do.

Many achieved their goal of sending money home to their families, and some were able to return to their home villages in China to resume their lives. Their local legacy is clear: they helped build a vibrant economy in a small county in Northern California that today is known around the world for its climate, its scenic vistas and its wine. They gave so much to the Napa Valley, and they should be remembered and honored for their hard work and sacrifice.

APPENDIX

TABLE 5. OCCUPATIONS OF CHINESE WORKERS IN NAPA COUNTY, 1870.

Occupation	Napa	Yountville	St. Helena	Grand Total
Laborer	58	-	46	104
Domestic Servant	47	4	5	56
Works in Hop Yard	-	-	44	44
Laundry	33	-	10	43
Cook	2	3	5	10
At Home	1	-	1	2
Railroad	-	-	2	2
Works in Tannery	1	-	-	1
Total	**142**	**7**	**113**	**262**

Source: 1870 U.S. Census for Napa County. In the census, Yountville was recorded as Yount Township. St. Helena was recorded as Hot Springs.

TABLE 6. OCCUPATIONS OF CHINESE WORKERS IN NAPA COUNTY, 1880.

Occupation	Napa	Yountville	St. Helena	Calistoga	Knox	Monticello	Total
Laborer	61	79	135	-	-	5	280
Cook	84	22	46	8	3	1	164
Railroad	98	-	-	-	-	-	98
Tannery	61	-	-	-	-	-	61
Laundry	44	2	2	5	1	1	55
Domestic Servant	28	1	14	-	2	-	45
Miner	-	-	-	-	42	-	42
Vineyard Worker	-	-	24	-	-	-	24
Grocery/ Merchant	6	-	16	-	-	-	22
"Insane"	19	-	2	-	-	-	21
Farm Laborer	21	-	-	-	-	-	21
Gardener	14	-	3	-	-	-	17
Farm Cook	11	-	-	-	-	-	11
N/A	7	1	-	-	-	-	8
Waiter	4	-	-	1	-	-	5
Wine Cellar	4	-	1	-	-	-	5
Dishwasher	2	-	-	-	-	-	2
Barber	-	-	2	-	-	-	2
Tailor	1	-	-	-	-	-	1
Doctor	-	-	1	-	-	-	1
Total	**465**	**105**	**246**	**14**	**48**	**7**	**885**

Source: 1880 U.S. Census for Napa County. Yountville was recorded as Yount Township. St. Helena was recorded as Hot Springs. Knox and Monticello refer to towns no longer present.

TABLE 7. POPULATION OF CHINESE CHILDREN IN NAPA COUNTY, 1881–1899.[339]

	1881	1883	1887	1890	1893	1896	1898	1899
Girls (ages 5–17)	-	-	-	1	1	2	2	2
Boys (ages 5–17)	-	-	-	-	3	5	3	7
Girls and Boys (under 5)	-	-	-	5	3	2	4	6
Girls and Boys (under 17)	4	23	12	-	-	-	-	-
Total	**4**	**23**	**12**	**6**	**7**	**9**	**10**	**15**

Prior to 1890, Chinese children were not allowed to attend public schools and were not distinguished by ages between school age and non–school age.
Sources: Various Napa County newspapers.

NOTES

Introduction

1. Visit Napa Valley, "Travel Research & Statistics," https://www.visitnapavalley.com/about-us/research.
2. See Ngai, *Impossible Subjects*.
3. U.S. Congress, "Report of the Joint Special Committee," 667.
4. Heintz, *California's Napa Valley*, 174–76.
5. The city of Napa does have one small parklet and a few plaques on a downtown bridge that acknowledge the presence, but not the contributions, of its Chinese residents.
6. Smith and Elliott, *Illustrations of Napa County, California*, 5. Note that Napa County consists of the Napa Valley plus a smaller valley to the west, Pope Valley. I will refer to Napa Valley where possible, but sometimes I will need to discuss the entire Napa County, as many statistics, such as the U.S. Census figures, are compiled at the county level. Since the towns in Napa Valley constituted the vast majority of the population of the county and its economic output, the difference is negligible.
7. The relative sizes and characterizations of the towns pertain to how they were in the late 1800s, although it remains true today.
8. Chinn, Lai and Choy, *History of the Chinese in California*, 70–71.
9. Wang, *United States and China*, 89.
10. Ngai, *Impossible Subjects*, 19. It is important to point out that other groups, notably African Americans, suffered unimaginable discrimination and depravation for years prior to the arrival of Chinese immigrants. The Chinese example here is only in relation to anti-immigration legislation.

Chapter 1

11. Chan, *This Bittersweet Soil*, 16–25.
12. See Jung, *Coolies and Cane*.
13. Wang, *United States and China*, 75.
14. Johnson, *Roaring Camp*, 243–46.
15. Chan, *This Bittersweet Soil*, 37–38.
16. Nordoff, *California*, 90.
17. Street, *Beasts of the Field*, 38–40.
18. Ibid., 137–38.
19. Ibid., 164–65.
20. Loomis, "How Our Chinamen Are Employed," 231–39.
21. Chiu, *Chinese Labor in California*, 69–72.
22. Heintz, *California's Napa Valley*, 82.
23. "An Outside Opinion; A 'Post' Correspondent on St. Helena Wines," *St. Helena Star*, December 19, 1879, 1.
24. Street, *Beasts of the Field*, 315.
25. Sources: Values for 1860, 1870 and 1880: 1880 U.S. Census, Population by Race, Sex and Nativity, page 382. Values for 1890 and 1900: 1910 U.S. Census, Bulletin 127, Chinese and Japanese in the United States 1910, table 58, page 36. The change in ratio is illustrative because in absolute terms, the Chinese population never surpassed 10 percent of the white population in the county. However, the rapid growth of the Chinese population, especially between 1870 and 1880, must have been shocking to a population likely primed to be biased against Chinese people.
26. This section is summarized from Jue, "Jue Joe Clan History," and related pages within that website.
27. Chinn, Lai and Choy, *History of the Chinese in California*, 64–66.

Chapter 2

28. Bancroft, *Works of Hubert Howe Bancroft*, 241.
29. There are a variety of limitations using U.S. Census results from this period, but it still has value in understanding the kinds of occupations in which the Chinese were engaged. Even with an incomplete dataset, we can ascertain details and trends that can greatly aid in our understanding of the economic contributions the Chinese made to the Napa Valley.
30. Stevenson, *Silverado Squatters*, 16.
31. Menefee, *Historical and Descriptive Sketch Book*, 215.
32. Heintz, *Wine Country*, 131.
33. "Winemaking in Napa; How the Work Is Done at Krug's Great Winery," *St. Helena Star*, October 19, 1883, 1.
34. Haraszthy, "Wine-Making in California, Part II," 41.
35. Chang et al., *Chinese and the Iron Road*, 284.
36. Heintz, *California's Napa Valley*, 87.

37. Street, *Beasts of the Field*, 317.
38. Chang et al., *Chinese and the Iron Road*, 149.
39. Street, *Beasts of the Field*, 316.
40. "Farmer's Club," *Napa Valley Register*, November 16, 1872, 1.
41. Street, *Beasts of the Field*, 280.
42. Menefee, *Historical and Descriptive Sketch Book*, 217.
43. Heintz, *California's Napa Valley*, 121.
44. "Rutherford Items," *St. Helena Star*, September 30, 1887, 3.
45. Street, *Beasts of the Field*, 319–22.
46. Hilgard, "Future of Grape-Growing in California," 1–6.
47. Sheldon, "Chinese Immigration Discussion," 113–19, 115–16.
48. Street, *Beasts of the Field*, 317–19. Ironically, while the treatment of Chinese in the Napa Valley may have led to the development of the section of the state constitution establishing anti-Chinese laws as a foundation of 1880 California, it was another Napa Valley business, a quicksilver mine, that challenged that section and had it stricken from the state constitution.
49. "Vineyard Labor; The Wages Demanded by Chinese Workers," *St. Helena Star*, June 9, 1884, 1.
50. The bunkhouse is currently used for storage, so pictures of the inside are not indicative of how it would have looked in the nineteenth century. The outside appears unchanged from the late 1800s.
51. The description of the contributions of the Chinese laborers, pictures from the Schramsberg Archives and pictures taken on-site at Schramsberg are courtesy of Hugh Davies, owner of Schramsberg Winery, and Matthew Levy, marketing manager. Visit took place on September 30, 2021.
52. "Nixon and Zhou's 'Toast to Peace,'" *Weekly Calistogian*, March 15, 2012.
53. "Among Our Hop Growers," *St. Helena Star*, August 11, 1884, 3.
54. "Hops. St. Helena's Product in That Line," *St. Helena Star*, September 29, 1876, 3.
55. "Hops. The Yield in St. Helena," *St. Helena Star*, August 3, 1877, 3.
56. Wallace and Kanaga, *1901 History of Napa County*, 90.
57. "Eastern Advices of the 5th State that Hops Are Up in That Market...," *Napa County Reporter*, August 11, 1882, 4.
58. "Local," *St. Helena Star*, September 1, 1876, 2.
59. "Hop Picking," *St. Helena Star*, September 11, 1884, 3.
60. "The Healdsberg Flag Says that Over 1000 Persons Are Employed...," *St. Helena Star*, September 15, 1884, 3.
61. "An Agent Has Been through Sonoma and Mendocino Counties Arranging for the Employment...," *St. Helena Star*, March 9, 1885, 3.
62. "Keep the Money at Home," *St. Helena Star*, September 2, 1887, 3.
63. "Praise for Mr. Dowdell," *Napa Register* October 14, 1892, 6.
64. "Chinese Hop Pickers Are Very Slick Individuals...," *Napa Journal*, August 30, 1893, 3.
65. Wallace and Kanaga, *1901 History of Napa County*, 110.
66. Ransome, "Our Mineral Supplies—Quicksilver," 210–17.

67. *History of Napa and Lake Counties, California*, 158–79.

68. "Quicksilver," *St. Helena Star*, March 12, 1880, 2.

69. Wallace and Kanaga, *1901 History of Napa County*, 118.

70. "A Fearful Explosion at the Oathill Quicksilver Mine in Chinatown," *Weekly Calistogian*, April 22, 1898, 3.

71. "Quicksilver," *St. Helena Star*, March 12, 1880, 2.

72. "Up Valley News," *Napa Valley Register*, February 27, 1880, 3.

73. "Chinamen Discharged," *Napa Valley Register*, February 27, 1880, 3.

74. "The Sulphur Bank Mine Is Discharging the Chinamen," *St. Helena Star*, March 12, 1880, 2.

75. "An Unconstitutional Anti-Chinese Law," *Napa Valley Register*, March 23, 1880, 2.

76. "Work Resumed," *Napa Valley Register*, March 25, 1880, 3.

77. Wallace and Kanaga, *1901 History of Napa County*, 164.

78. The names don't make any sense together, but apparently those were the names of the two camps and both contained Chinese miners.

79. Goss, *Life and Death of a Quicksilver Mine*, 65–66.

80. Ibid., 136.

81. "Calistoga," *St. Helena Star*, May 7, 1886, 1.

82. "Local Briefs," *Napa Valley Register*, February 19, 1880, 3.

83. Goss, *Life and Death of a Quicksilver Mine*, 66.

84. Ibid., 67–70.

85. Ibid., 73.

86. U.S. EPA, OCSPP, "Health Effects of Exposures to Mercury."

87. "A Fearful Explosion at the Oathill Quicksilver Mine in Chinatown," *Weekly Calistogian*, April 22, 1898, 3.

88. Heintz, *California's Napa Valley*, 88.

89. "Fire! Fire," *St. Helena Star*, July 29, 1875, 3.

90. "Chinese Wages," *St. Helena Star*, January 5, 1877, 2.

91. "Local," *St. Helena Star*, June 8, 1877, 3.

92. "Incendiarism," *St. Helena Star*, November 15, 1878, 3.

93. *Daily Alta California*, July 23, 1863, quoted in Chan, *This Bittersweet Soil*, 242.

94. Loomis, "How Our Chinamen Are Employed," 233.

95. McCormick, *Short History of Grandfather York*, 12–13. Author's note: John York is my great-great-great-grandfather.

96. Wang, *United States and China*, 75.

97. Chang et al., *Chinese and the Iron Road*, 280.

98. Bischoff, Sterner and Thompson, "Napa River Railroad Bridge," 8.

99. 1880 U.S. Census for Napa, 358 and 368.

100. *Napa Register*, October 23, 1883, 3.

101. "There Are 215 Chinamen Employed on the Rutherford and Clear Lake Railroad," *St. Helena Star*, September 3, 1886, 5.

102. "Napa City Reporter," *St. Helena Star*, September 24, 1886, 1.

103. "Calistogian Items," *St. Helena Star*, November 21, 1879, 2.

104. "Railroad," *Napa Valley Register*, October 25, 1880, 1.

Chapter 3

105. Yu, *Chinatown, San Jose, USA*, 63.
106. "Odds," *St. Helena Star*, May 20, 1875, 2.
107. "Local," *St. Helena Star*, February 8, 1878, 3.
108. "Ginger, the Chinese Merchant of This Place, Has Failed to the Tune of $1,000," *St. Helena Star*, August 30, 1878, 3.
109. The *Napa Register* reprinted a joke from *LIFE* magazine in its July 22, 1892 edition: "He: I'm looking for a girl who can bake a cake, a loaf of bread, or cook a meal; one who isn't afraid to sew a button on, or soil her hands in a little housework. She: I should strongly advise you to try an intelligence office."
110. "Ordinance Number Two," *Napa County Reporter*, May 25, 1883, 3.
111. "Board of Trustees," *Napa County Reporter*, April 23, 1886, 3.
112. "New Advertisements," *St. Helena Star*, February 13, 1880, 3.
113. "China New Years Was Duly Celebrated Here, Ending with a Grand Firing of Crackers and Bombs," *St. Helena Star*, February 11, 1881, 1.
114. "A Big Blaze," *St. Helena Star*, August 14, 1884, 3.
115. Wong, *Gum Sahn Yun*, 143–48.
116. "Story of a Distinguished Napa Family," *Napa Register*, June 21, 1961, 3.
117. Chiu, *Chinese Labor in California*, 89–128.
118. True Nappa leather is typically only offered on high-end models of car brands like BMW, Porsche and Rolls-Royce. Cars, "What Is Nappa Leather?," https://www.cars.com/articles/what-is-nappa-leather-432078.
119. The Hide & Leather House Inc., "The History Behind Napa Valley's Tanning Industry," https://www.hidehouse.com/content/napa-tannery-history.asp.
120. *History of Napa and Lake Counties, California*, 279–80.
121. U.S. Census Record, Napa, California, 289–90.
122. "The Anti-Chinese Movement," *Napa County Reporter*, February 5, 1886, 2.
123. Stevenson, *Silverado Squatters*, 74.
124. McLeod, *Pigtails and Gold Dust*, 100.
125. Letter from W.W. Hyman, dated May 1964, courtesy of the St. Helena Historical Society.
126. The occupations listed in the census regarding laundry work were vague. The descriptions included terms or phrases like "works in laundry," "laundryman" and "laundry," and they seemed to be used interchangeably to describe employment in this area.
127. "Women's Protective League," *Napa County Reporter*, July 14, 1882, 4.
128. "French Laundry," *Napa Valley Register*, June 14, 1880, 3.
129. 1883 Napa County Ordinance II, Section VIII—Laundry Tax.
130. "St. Helena Cries Loudly for the Clear-Headed, Enterprising Individual," *St. Helena Star*, January 22, 1885, 2.
131. "The White Laundry," *St. Helena Star*, March 12, 1885, 3.
132. "Napa Steam Laundry," *Napa Register*, November 6, 1885, 3.
133. "The White Laundry," *Napa Register*, January 29, 1886, 1.

134. "An Excellent Project," *Napa County Reporter* February 5, 1886, 1.
135. "White Laundry!," *Napa Register*, March 5, 1886, 2.
136. "Quong He Fat Choy!," *Napa County Reporter*, February 20, 1885, 4.
137. Caselaw Access Project, "In Re Sam Kee, 31 F. 680 (1887)," https://cite.case. law/f/31/680.
138. "Superior Court," *Napa Weekly Journal*, April 21, 1887, 3.
139. "The Laundry Ordinance Declared Unconstitutional," *Napa Weekly Journal*, May 5, 1887, 3.
140. Caselaw Access Project, "Citations to In Re Sam Kee, 31 F. 680 (1887)," https://cite.case.law/citations/?q=3761404.
141. McClain, *In Search of Equality*, 331–32.
142. "City Marshall Deweese Yesterday Arrested Sam Kee," *Napa Weekly Journal*, June 16, 1887, 3.
143. "Pulpit Paragraphs," *Napa Register*, June 24, 1887, 1.
144. "Local Briefs," *Napa Register*, July 8, 1887, 3.
145. Wallace and Kanaga, *1901 History of Napa County*, 201.
146. "Chinese Laundry Removed," *Napa Journal*, October 25, 1907, 3.
147. Chan, *This Bittersweet Soil*, 86.
148. Ibid., 142.
149. "Ordinance No. 50," *Napa Valley Register*, May 13, 1880, 1.
150. "Town Trustees Meet," *St. Helena Star*, February 18, 1898, 3.
151. "The Anti-Chinese League," *Napa Register*, March 26, 1886, 1.
152. "Up Valley Items," *Napa Register*, March 5, 1886, 2.
153. "It Is Estimated There Are 300 Chinese Vegetable Peddlers in Los Angeles," *Napa County Reporter*, April 18, 1890, 6.
154. "Local Briefs," *Napa Register*, April 24, 1885, 1.
155. "Cutting Scrape Near St. Helena," *Napa County Reporter*, August 28, 1885, 3.
156. "Chan Ah Lai, a Chinese Vegetable Peddler of Napa," *St. Helena Star*, May 27, 1887, 5.

Chapter 4

157. 1880 U.S. Census sheet, Napa City in the County of Napa, 323 and 324.
158. Ibid., 293 and 296. Sixty-three were counted as working in the tannery, and two were counted as cooks.
159. *History of Napa and Lake Counties*, 235.
160. *Chinatown—Sam Brannan E Clampus Vitus Chapter 1004*, Napa, California, August 18, 1979. This is a newsletter documenting a ceremony honoring Shuck Chan, son of one of the earliest residents of Napa's Chinatown, Chan Wah Jack.
161. "Story of a Distinguished Napa Family," *Napa Register*, June 21, 1961, 3.
162. See the discussion of religion in chapter 4 for a more complete description of Joss Houses.

163. "Chinatown Burns," *Napa Journal,* January 30, 1902, 3.
164. This was his second marriage. His first wife, known only by her family name, Lee, died shortly after they married.
165. "The Battery Case," *Napa Journal,* May 14, 1904, 3.
166. "Mrs. Chan Wah Jack Sacrifices Home for Napa's Welfare," *Napa Journal,* April 8, 1930. 1.
167. "Napa Chinese Now Lawyer," *Napa Journal,* May 19, 1919, 5.
168. "Big Event, Arrival of Blue Blooded Chinese Baby Causes Much Ado in Celestial Quarter," *Napa Journal,* March 24, 1909, 2.
169. Ezettie, "Looking into Napa's Past and Present."
170. "Shuck Hing Buys Café in Boston," *Napa Journal,* September 4, 1919, 5; "Back from China," *Napa Weekly Journal,* January 29, 1909, 2.
171. Street, *Beasts of the Field,* 345.
172. "Mr. Gillam's Letter—A Property Owner in His Own Defence—A Bit of History Regarding Chinatown," *St. Helena Star,* February 12, 1886, 2.
173. Weber, *Old Napa Valley,* 198.
174. "Anti-Chinese—St. Helena's Protest Against the Chinamen," *St. Helena Star,* December 4, 1885, 3.
175. "Opium Fiends," *St. Helena Star,* December 18, 1885, 2.
176. Weber, *Old Napa Valley,* 200.
177. "Mr. Gillam's Letter," 2.
178. "Town Trustees," *St. Helena Star,* January 21, 1881, 3.
179. "Board of Health," *St. Helena Star,* May 8, 1884, 3.
180. "A Big Blaze," *St. Helena Star,* August 14, 1884, 3.
181. "Mr. Gillam's Letter," 2.
182. "Chinatown Sold," *St. Helena Star,* February 19, 1886, 3.
183. "To the Citizens of St. Helena," *St. Helena Star,* April 9, 1886, 2.
184. "Chinatown Destroyed," *St. Helena Star,* October 20, 1911, 5.
185. "Rutherford Items," *St. Helena Star,* September 9, 1881, 3.
186. "Yung Him, of Rutherford, Is an Enterprising Celestial," *St. Helena Star,* July 3, 1884, 3.
187. "Yung Him, Proprietor of the Rutherford Employment Office," *St. Helena Star,* September 4, 1884, 3.
188. "Inquest," *Napa Register,* August 16, 1899, 2.
189. "Thomas Mark, the Enterprising Rutherford Cooper," *St. Helena Star,* April 12, 1895, 3.
190. Archuleta, *Early Calistoga,* 67–68.
191. Stevenson, *Silverado Squatters,* 74–75.
192. "Up Valley Items," *Napa Register,* March 30, 1883, 3.
193. Harley, "Letter from W.N. Harley to S.W. Collins."
194. "Calistoga Happenings," *Napa Journal,* June 14, 1914, 8.
195. "Calistoga Happenings," *Napa Journal,* March 28, 1915, 8.
196. "Chinese at War," *Napa County Reporter,* June 9, 1890, 2.

197. The only mention of Yountville's Chinese residents is a passing remark that "[o]n Hopper Creek stood what there was of a Chinatown in old Yountville: a laundry, tenement, and employment office for day laborers, called the China house." Dillon, *Napa Valley Heyday*, 183.

198. "Chinatown in a Colorful Area," *Napa Valley Register*, March 30, 1963, 78.

Chapter 5

199. Chinn, Lai and Choy, *History of the Chinese in California*, 15.

200. Cloud and Galenson, "Chinese Immigration and Contract Labor," 22–42. According to the article, the average monthly wage of a Chinese worker in China was $3 to $5 per month, and the cost of trans-Pacific passage was $40 to $50. Since vineyard workers could make $1 to $1.50 per day in Napa and miners even more, the economic tradeoff was compelling for these workers.

201. Cloud and Galenson, "Chinese Immigration and Contract Labor," 28.

202. Chung, "Between Two Worlds," 217–38.

203. Ibid., 235.

204. "Chinese Free Masonry," *St. Helena Star*, March 13, 1884, 1.

205. "Brevities," *Napa Reporter*, November 28, 1884, 3.

206. "John's New Year," *Napa Register*, January 24, 1890, 3.

207. "Petty Larceny," *St. Helena Star*, June 16, 1884, 3.

208. "Mixon & Son Have Just Completed a Joss House," *St. Helena Star*, June 5, 1891, 3.

209. "Happy Celestials," *St. Helena Star*, October 2, 1891, 3. The claim of the percentage of Chinese members of the Free Masons is based on a reported Chinese population of 875 in the 1890 census. Since the overall census numbers were likely undercounted and the self-reported Free Mason membership could have certainly been exaggerated, the exact percentage of Chinese residents that were Free Masons is likely impossible to determine. Regardless, it was a significant percentage of the Chinese population.

210. Chung, "Between Two Worlds," 222–23.

211. Ibid., 224.

212. Almost every newspaper article about a Chinese funeral procession complained about the volume (too loud) and quality (very low) of the Chinese band that accompanied the mourners. Unfortunately, we have no way of objectively determining if the Chinese band played their music well or not. It clearly did not match the taste of Napa Valley's white residents at the time.

213. "Chinese Funeral," *St. Helena Star*, April 7, 1884, 3.

214. "A Chinese Funeral," *Napa Journal*, February 15, 1899, 3.

215. "Killed by a Falling Tree," *St. Helena Star*, January 12, 1894, 3.

216. Chung, "Between Two Worlds," 218.

217. Tulocay Cemetery, "Cemetery Tours," https://www.tulocaycemetery.org/cemetery-tours.

218. Brennan, "Dead Men and Women Do Tell Tales."

219. Yu, *Chinatown, San Jose, USA*, 51.
220. McLeod, *Pigtails and Gold Dust*, 294.
221. "Chinatown," *Napa Register*, February 29, 1884, 1.
222. "A Continued Look at Chinatown," *Napa Valley Register*, January 28, 1996, 22.
223. The banner at the top of the shrine "北極殿" means Temple of the "Bei-Ji" God. The outer poem, "神靈居北坎 帝德耀南離," praises the powerful and encompassing ancient God. The inner poem, "北極尊無極 南天別有天," reminds people of the infinity and that there are universes beyond this one. Many thanks to Lee Liu Chin for her interpretation and description of the beautiful altar.
224. U.S. Congress, "Report of the Joint Special Committee," 490.
225. "Chinese Chapel," *Napa Register*, February 10, 1883, 1.
226. "Sunday Evening a Crowd of Boys and Young Men," *Napa County Reporter*, February 23, 1883, 4.
227. *Napa Register*, February 1, 1884, 3. Note that this is the same Richard Wylie discussed in chapter 3 regarding Chinatowns. He and his wife had a Chinese servant who lived with them.
228. "The Chinese Sunday School," *Napa County Reporter*, October 24, 1884, 3.
229. "The Chinese New Year," *Napa Register*, February 8, 1889, 1.
230. All Souls Day is celebrated on the fourteenth day of the seventh month in the lunar calendar.
231. "From Saturday's Daily," *Napa Register*, September 21, 1883, 1.
232. "Chinese New Year," *St. Helena Star*, February 13, 1880, 3.
233. "Although Chinese New Year Is Passing Off Quietly," *St. Helena Star*, January 31, 1884, 3.
234. "Chinese New Year Commenced Monday," *St. Helena Star*, February 1, 1889, 3.
235. "County News," *St. Helena Star*, February 11, 1884, 1.
236. "Rutherford Items," *St. Helena Star*, February 17, 1882, 3.
237. "The Chinese New Year," *Napa Register*, February 8, 1889, 1.
238. "Chinese Festivities," *Napa Register*, February 10, 1880, 3.
239. Goss, *Life and Death of a Quicksilver Mine*, 81–82.
240. Chan, *This Bittersweet Soil*, 386–91.
241. "Chinese Wedding," *Napa County Reporter*, September 25, 1885, 3.
242. "Two Chinese Couple," *St. Helena Star*, December 11, 1885, 3.
243. "Ah Set Fon, Who Has Been Teaching English," *St. Helena Star*, April 14, 1882, 2.
244. "Our Man About Town," *Napa County Reporter*, March 21, 1884, 1.
245. "Town and Country," *Napa County Reporter*, October 24, 1884, 3.
246. "Chinese Mission School," *St. Helena Star*, October 29, 1886, 5.

Chapter 6

247. Chin, "'Chinaman's Chance' in Court," 965–90.
248. McClain, *In Search of Equality*, 20–23.
249. *People v. Jones*, 31 Cal. 566, 574 (1867), as quoted in Chin, "'Chinaman's Chance' in Court," 969.

250. McClain, *In Search of Equality*, 38. Interestingly, the addition of this section was driven almost exclusively by Senator William Stewart of Nevada, who had spent considerable time in the mining districts of California and saw the level of discrimination Chinese faced there on a daily basis. There was no requirement in the text of the Fifteenth Amendment to extend civil rights protection to the Chinese.

251. McClain, *In Search of Equality*, 41.

252. "If There Is One Thing Remarks an Exchange," *Napa County Reporter*, February 25, 1887, 2.

253. *People v. Foo*, 44 P. 453, 455–56 (Cal. 1896), as quoted in Chin, "'Chinaman's Chance' in Court," 971.

254. "For Assaulting Chinamen," *Napa Register*, May 6, 1887, 3.

255. "Petty Larceny," *St. Helena Star*, June 16, 1884, 3.

256. "Not Acceptable," *St. Helena Star*, November 26, 1874, 2.

257. Yu, *Chinatown, San Jose, USA*, 59.

258. "The Vile and Vicious Habit of Opium," *Napa Valley Register*, March 11, 1880, 3.

259. "Editorial Notes," *Napa County Reporter*, January 14, 1881, 2.

260. "Morphomania," *Napa County Reporter*, February 17, 1882, 1.

261. "Ordinance No. 98," *Napa County Reporter*, January 7, 1881, 4.

262. "Raid on the Opium Dens," *Napa County Reporter*, May 20, 1881, 3.

263. "Superior Court—Wallace, Judge," *Napa County Reporter*, June 30, 1882, 1.

264. *Napa County Reporter*, July 7, 1882, 1. While Ah Louie was quoted in the paper, the quote, as was typical of the time, was rendered in a mocking English prose that was supposed to phonetically mimic a Chinese accent. Ah Louie's quote was rendered as "Ah, ya, me no sabe, Glidley he no like Chinaman" (referring to Judge Gridley, who presided over the proceeding).

265. "Opium Smokers Take Warning," *Napa County Reporter*, November 24, 1882, 3.

266. "Mongolian Opium Smokers," *Napa County Reporter*, March 26, 1886, 1.

267. "Good for St. Helena," *St. Helena Star*, October 30, 1885, 1.

268. "A Chinaman Suicides," *Napa Register*, June 1, 1888, 3.

269. Ahmad, *Opium Debate*, 77–83.

270. Culin, *Gambling Games of the Chinese in America*, 15–16.

271. "A Large Meeting, Resolutions Adopted and an Anti-Chinese Club Organized," *Napa Register*, February 12, 1886, 3. See chapter 7 for a more extensive discussion of the Napa Anti-Chinese League.

272. "Chinese Gambling," *Napa Journal*, February 21, 1894, 4.

273. Goss, *Life and Death of a Quicksilver Mine*, 78–79.

274. "Ordinance No. 23," *Napa Valley Register*, May 4, 1880, 4.

275. "The Chinese Gambling Cases," *Napa Valley Register*, April 8, 1880, 3.

276. "Chinese 'Tan' Players Arrested," *Napa Register*, February 20, 1885, 1.

277. "Anti-Chinese, St. Helena's Protest Against the Chinamen," *St. Helena Star*, December 4, 1885, 3.

278. "Ordinance No. 47," *St. Helena Star*, June 22, 1883, 2.

279. Interestingly, this location is not in Chinatown proper, but downtown St. Helena, possibly to make it easier for white townspeople to visit.
280. "Another Gambling Raid on the Chinese," *St. Helena Star*, August 3, 1883, 3.
281. "Shooting Affray," *St. Helena Star*, July 12, 1889, 3.
282. "Killed," *St. Helena Star*, January 21, 1875, 3.
283. "Murder," *Napa Journal*, October 31, 1894, 3.
284. "Local Briefs," *Napa Journal*, January 19, 1895, 3.
285. "Out Twelve Hours," *Napa Register*, January 25, 1895, 1.
286. Women were not allowed to serve on a California jury until 1917.

Chapter 7

287. Sandmeyer, *Anti-Chinese Movement in California*, 15.
288. Sources: Figures from 1860 and 1870: Sandmeyer, Anti-Chinese Movement in California, 17. Figures from 1880, 1890 and 1900: 1910 U.S. Census, Bulletin 127, Chinese and Japanese in the United States 1910, table 53, page 25.
289. Ibid., 25–39.
290. Ibid., 41.
291. Ibid., 75.
292. "Anti-Chinese; The State Convention in San Jose," *Santa Cruz Sentinel*, February 6, 1886, 5.
293. "The Boycott; The Bone of Contention at the State Convention," *San Francisco Examiner*, March 12, 1886, 2.
294. "Anti-Chinese; St. Helena's Protest Against the Chinaman," *St. Helena Star*, December 4, 1885, 3.
295. Ibid.
296. "Anti-Coolieites; They Visit Chinatown in a Body," *St. Helena Star*, February 5, 1886, 3.
297. "The Chinese Problem; As Discussed by Leading Vineyardists," *St. Helena Star*, February 12, 1886, 3.
298. "The Chinese in St. Helena," *Napa Weekly Journal*, February 11, 1886, 3.
299. "Anti-Chinese Meeting," *Napa Weekly Journal*, February 11, 1886, 3.
300. "The Citizens of Sacramento and the Anti-Chinese League of San Jose," *Napa County Reporter*, January 29, 1886, 2. There were competing statewide anti-Chinese conventions being organized in early 1886. There was one in early February organized by the San Jose Anti-Chinese League, which was based on aggregating local Anti-Chinese League groups from around the state. The Sacramento one being held in March focused on representation from each county, regardless of whether it had a formal Anti-Chinese League or not.
301. "A Good Move," *Napa Weekly Journal*, March 11, 1886, 3.
302. "The League Meeting," *Napa Register*, March 19, 1886, 1.
303. "Anti-Chinese League," *Napa County Reporter*, February 26, 1886, 3.
304. "Anti-Chinese League," *Napa Weekly Journal*, March 4, 1886, 3.

305. "Not a Wise Move," *Napa County Reporter*, March 12, 1886, 2.

306. "The League Meeting," *Napa Register*, March 19, 1886, 1.

307. "The Boycott," *Napa Register*, March 26, 1886, 2.

308. "At the Meeting of the Anti-Chinese League Saturday Evening," *Napa Weekly Journal*, April 22, 1886, 3.

309. "Do Unto Others, etc.," *Napa Register*, April 23, 1886, 2.

310. "Will It Work?," *Napa Register*, May 28, 1886, 1.

311. "A Two-Edged Plaything," *Napa Weekly Journal*, May 27, 1886, 2.

312. "Will Do It for Pay," *Napa County Reporter*, May 28, 1886, 2.

313. "The Blighted Boycott," *Napa Register*, May 28, 1886, 2.

314. "Local Briefs," *Napa Register*, May 28, 1886, 3.

315. "There Was Quite a Large Audience at Phoenix Hall," *Napa County Reporter*, June 18, 1886, 1.

316. "The Anti-Chinese League," *Napa Weekly Journal*, June 17, 1886, 3.

317. "The Anti-Chinese War," *San Francisco Chronicle*, November 9, 1886.

318. "Anti-Chinese League," *Napa County Reporter*, February 26, 1886, 3.

319. "White Labor Union," *St. Helena Star*, August 25, 1893, 3.

320. "Calistoga," *Napa Register*, October 13, 1893, 4.

321. "Greystone Sold," *St. Helena Star*, June 1, 1884, 3.

322. "Fruit Growers Should Inspect the Trees at Napa Valley Nurseries," *Napa Journal*, February 19, 1893, 3.

323. "A Voice from 'The Other Side,'" *Napa Register*, February 12, 1886, 1.

324. Pfaelzer, *Driven Out*, 123.

Conclusion

325 Sources: Chinese values for 1870 and 1880: 1880 U.S. Census, Population by Race, Sex, and Nativity, page 382. Values for 1890 and 1900: 1910 U.S. Census, Bulletin 127, Chinese and Japanese in the United States 1910, table 58, page 36. Italian values for 1870, 1890, 1900 and 1910: Hans Christian Palmer, "Italian Immigration and the Development of California Agriculture" (PhD, University of California, Berkeley), Table XXXVII. Values for 1920: 1920 U.S. Census, Volume 3, Population, page 124. Source for Italian population of Napa County, 1880: author's manual compilation.

326. "Friday, August 4, Being the Day on Which the Anti-Chinese Law Takes Effect," *St. Helena Star*, August 4, 1882, 2.

327. Wang, *United States and China*, 78-82.

328. "Old Chinatown," *Napa Valley Register*, April 1988, 4.

329. "Napa Organizes for Drive to Clean Up Riverfront," *Napa Journal*, April 8, 1930, 1.

330. "Wayside Notes," *Napa Valley Register*, April 29, 1880, 3.

331. "Lorenzo Carbone—Old and Highly Esteemed Pioneer Answers Death's Call," *Napa Journal*, January 31, 1908, 1. Author's note: Lorenzo Carbone was my great-great-grandfather. According to family lore, the three Carbone brothers left Genoa to escape a murder charge, which was later dropped.

332. California Board of State Viticultural Commissioners, "Annual Report of the Board of State Viticultural Commissioners for 1889–1890," 15–16.
333. Ibid., 48.
334. Heintz, *California's Napa Valley*, 170–74.
335. Simpson, *Creating Wine*, 199–200.
336. Heintz, *California's Napa Valley*, 176.
337. Sam Brannan #1004 ECV, "What Is E Clampus Vitus," September 26, 2021, https://www.clamper.com.
338. "Chinatown Ceremonies Honor Chan," *Napa Valley Register*, August 20, 1979, 2.

Appendix

339. Sources: Figures from 1881: "School Census Marshal's Report," *Napa County Reporter*, June 3, 1881, 3. Figures from 1883: "School Statistics of Napa County," *Napa County Reporter*, July 13, 1883, 3. Figures from 1887: "The School Census," *Napa Weekly Journal*, June 30, 1887, 3. Figures from 1890: "School Census, Some Interesting Figures Concerning Our School Population," *Napa Journal*, June 13, 1890, 3. Figures from 1893: "A Good Showing, Is Made by the School Census Marshall of This District," *Napa Register*, May 26, 1893, 3. Figures from 1896: "Increase of Population, in Napa School District Census Marshall's Report," *Napa Register*, May 8, 1896, 1. Figures from 1898: "County School Census," *Napa Journal*, June 29, 1898, 3. Figures from 1899: "County School Census," *St. Helena Star*, June 23, 1899, 2.

BIBLIOGRAPHY

Newspapers

Napa County Reporter.
Napa Daily Register.
Napa Journal.
Napa Register/Napa Valley Register.
Napa Weekly Journal.
San Francisco Chronicle.
Santa Cruz Sentinel.
St. Helena Star.
Weekly Calistogian.

Sources

Ahmad, Diana L. *The Opium Debate and Chinese Exclusion Laws in the Nineteenth-Century American West*. Reno: University of Nevada Press, 2007. https://catalog.hathitrust. org/Record/005557734.

Archuleta, Kay. *Early Calistoga: The Brannen Saga*. Calistoga, CA: Illuminations Press, 1977.

Bancroft, Hubert Howe. *The Works of Hubert Howe Bancroft: Essays and Miscellany, 1890*. N.p.: History Company, 1890.

Bickford, Elmer. *Chinese Youth at Chinese New Year*. February 19, 1896. Photograph. 1979.27.1b. Napa County Historical Society.

Bischoff, Matt C., Matthew A Sterner and Scott Thompson. "Napa River Railroad Bridge—Photographs, Written Historical and Descriptive Data." Department of the Interior, April 2003. HAER No. CA-322.

Brennan, Nancy S. "Dead Men and Women Do Tell Tales: Chinese Families at Napa's Tulocay Cemetery." *Napa Valley Register*, July 5, 2018. https://napavalleyregister.com/lifestyles/dead-men-and-women-do-tell-tales-chinese-families-at-napas-tulocay-cemetery/article_2f061a2f-49ce-5b77-b3f3-b0c5f45d5dc9.html.

Brown, Alexandria. *Hidden History of Napa Valley*. Charleston, SC: The History Press, 2019.

California Board of State Viticultural Commissioners. "Annual Report of the Board of State Viticultural Commissioners for 1889–1890." Sacramento, California, 1890.

Chang, Gordon H., Shelley Fisher Fishkin, Hilton Obenzinger and Roland Hsu. *The Chinese and the Iron Road: Building the Transcontinental Railroad*. Asian America. Stanford, CA: Stanford University Press, 2019.

Chan, Sucheng. *This Bittersweet Soil: The Chinese in California Agriculture, 1860–1910*. Berkeley: University of California Press, 1989.

Chin, Gabriel. "'A Chinaman's Chance' in Court: Asian Pacific Americans and Racial Rules of Evidence." *UC Irvine Law Review* 3, no. 4 (December 1, 2013): 965–90.

Chinn, Thomas. "Chinese in Napa." Chinese Historical Society of America Bulletin, 1966.

Chinn, Thomas W., H. Mark Lai and Phillip P. Choy, eds. *A History of the Chinese in California—A Syllabus*. 6th ed. San Francisco, CA: Chinese Historical Society of America, 1984.

Chiu, Ping. *Chinese Labor in California—An Economic Study*. Logmark Edition. Madison: Department of History, University of Wisconsin, 1967.

Chung, Sue Fawn. "Between Two Worlds: The Zhigongtang and Chinese American Funerary Rituals." In *The Chinese in America: A History from Gold Mountain to the New Millennium*, 217–38. Lanham, MD: Rowman & Littlefield, 2002.

Cloud, Patricia, and David W. Galenson. "Chinese Immigration and Contract Labor in the Late Nineteenth Century." *Explorations in Economic History* 24, no. 1 (January 1, 1987): 22–42. https://doi.org/10.1016/0014-4983(87)90003-9.

Coodley, Lauren. *Lost Napa Valley*. Charleston, SC: The History Press, 2021.

Culin, Stewart. *Chinese Games with Dice*. Philadelphia, PA: Franklin Printing Company, 1889. https://gallica.bnf.fr/ark:/12148/bpt6k375405s.

———. *The Gambling Games of the Chinese in America*. Philadelphia: University of Pennsylvania Press, 1891. http://www.chinacultureandsociety.amdigital.co.uk/Documents/Details/Z153_07_0456.

Daniels, Roger. *Asian America: Chinese and Japanese in the United States since 1850*. Seattle: University of Washington Press, 2011.

Dillingham, William P. *Reports of the Immigration Commission*. Vol. 4. Washington, D.C.: U.S. Government Printing Office, 1911.

Dillon, Richard. *Napa Valley Heyday*. N.p.: Book Club of California, 2004.

Ezettie, Louise. "Looking into Napa's Past and Present." *Napa Valley Register*, September 4, 1982.

Goss, Helen (Rocca). *The Life and Death of a Quicksilver Mine*. Los Angeles: Historical Society of Southern California, 1958. http://hdl.handle.net/2027/mdp.39015018022338.

Hansen, Mariam. "St. Helena's Chinese Heritage." St. Helena Historical Society, June 2011. https://shstory.org/st-helenaa-chinese-heritage.

Haraszthy, Arpad. "Wine-Making in California, Part II." *Overland Monthly* 8, no. 1 (January 1872): 34–41.

Harley, W.N. "Letter from W.N. Harley to S.W. Collins." October 4, 1896. Napa County Historical Society.

Heidenriech, Linda. "Elusive Citizenship: Education, the Press, and the Struggle Over Representation in Napa, California, 1848–1910." Chapter 2, in *Immigrant Life in the U.S.: Multi-Disciplinary Perspectives*. London: Routledge, 2004.

Heintz, William. *California's Napa Valley—One Hundred Sixty Years of Wine Making*. San Francisco, CA: Scottwell Associates, 1999.

———. *Wine Country: A History of Napa Valley, The Early Years: 1838–1920*. Santa Barbara, CA: Capra Press, 1990.

Hilgard, E.W. "The Future of Grape-Growing in California." *Overland Monthly* 3, no. 1 (January 1884): 1–6.

History of Napa and Lake Counties, California. N.p.: Slocum, Bowen & Company, 1881.

Johnson, Susan Lee. *Roaring Camp: The Social World of the California Gold Rush*. New York: W.W. Norton & Company, 2000.

Jue, Jack, Jr. "Jue Joe Clan History: Finding Our Roots—A Beginning." *Jue Joe Clan History* (blog), June 7, 2010. https://juejoeclan.blogspot.com/2010/06/finding-our-roots-beginning.html.

Jung, Moon Ho. *Coolies and Cane: Race, Labor, and Sugar in the Age of Emancipation*. Baltimore, MD: Johns Hopkins University Press, 2006.

Laube, James. "Napa Valley Wine Historian William Heintz Dies at 79." Wine Spectator, March 8, 2012. https://www.winespectator.com/articles/napa-valley-wine-historian-william-heintz-dies-at-79-46504.

Loomis, Reverend A.W. "How Our Chinamen Are Employed." *Overland Monthly* 2, no. 3 (March 1869): 231–39.

McClain, Charles J. *In Search of Equality—The Chinese Struggle Against Discrimination in Nineteenth-Century America*. Berkeley: University of California Press, 1994.

McCormick, Rodney. *A Short History of Grandfather York*. A Sketch from the Archives of the Napa County Historical Society 10. Napa, CA: Napa County Historical Society, 1938.

McLeod, Alexander. *Pigtails and Gold Dust*. Caldwell, ID: Caxton Printers, Ltd., 1947. https://catalog.hathitrust.org/Record/002965750.

McWilliams, Carey. *Factories in the Field: The Story of Migratory Farm Labor in California*. Berkeley: University of California Press, 1939.

Menefee, Campbell Augustus. *Historical and Descriptive Sketch Book of Napa, Sonoma, Lake and Mendocino, Comprising Sketches of Their Topography, Productions, History, Scenery, and Peculiar Attraction*. N.p.: Reporter Publishing House, 1873.

Ngai, Mae M. "Chinese Gold Miners and the 'Chinese Question' in Nineteenth-Century California and Victoria." *Journal of American History* (Bloomington, IN) 101, no. 4 (2015): 1,082–1,105.

———. *Impossible Subjects: Illegal Immigrants and the Making of Modern America*. New Paperback Edition. Princeton, NJ: Princeton University Press, 2014.

Nordoff, Charles. *California: A Book for Travelers and Settlers*. New York: Harper and Brothers, 1875.

Palmer, Hans Christian. "Italian Immigration and the Development of California Agriculture." PhD, University of California, Berkeley, 1965. https://www.proquest.com/docview/302132989/citation/93F13A545B2D48FAPQ/1.

Pfaelzer, Jean. *Driven Out—The Forgotten War Against Chinese Americans*. Berkeley: University of California Press, 2007.

Ransome, Frederick Leslie. "Our Mineral Supplies—Quicksilver." *USGS Bulletin*, 1919. https://doi.org/10.3133/b666FF.

Sandmeyer, Elmer Clarence. *The Anti-Chinese Movement in California*. Champaign: University of Illinois Press, 1939.

Saxton, Alexander. *The Indispensable Enemy: Labor and the Anti-Chinese Movement in California*. Berkeley: University of California Press, 1995.

Schudson, Michael. *Discovering the News: A Social History of American Newspapers*. New York: Basic Books, 1981.

Sheldon, Francis E. "The Chinese Immigration Discussion." *Overland Monthly* 7, no. 38 (February 1886): 113–19.

Simpson, James. *Creating Wine: The Emergence of a World Industry, 1840–1914*. 1st ed. Princeton, NJ: Princeton University Press, 2011.

Smith, Clarence L., and Wallace W. Elliott. *Illustrations of Napa County, California : With Historical Sketch*. Oakland, CA: Smith & Elliott, 1878. http://link.gale.com/apps/doc/CY0108244528/SABN?sid=bookmark-SABN&xid=e1c6231e&pg=5.

Stevenson, Robert Louis. *The Silverado Squatters*. London: Eveleigh Nash & Grayson, 1873.

Street, Richard Steven. *Beasts of the Field: A Narrative History of California Farmworkers, 1769–1913*. Stanford, CA: Stanford University Press, 2004.

Strong, M.H. *Young Chinese Men in Napa's Chinatown*. N.d. Photograph. 2012.2.99. Napa County Historical Society.

U.S. Census Bureau. "Availability of 1890 Census—History—U.S. Census Bureau." https://www.census.gov/history/www/genealogy/decennial_census_records/availability_of_1890_census.html.

———. "Census Supplement for California (1910)." N.d. https://www2.census.gov/library/publications/decennial/1910/abstract/supplement-ca.pdf.

———. "1880 Census: Volume 1. Statistics of the Population of the United States." Washington, D.C.: U.S. Government Printing Office, 1880. https://www2.census.gov/library/publications/decennial/1880/vol-01-population/1880_v1-13.pdf.

———. "1880 U.S. Census, Population by Race, Sex, and Nativity." Washington, D.C.: U.S. Government Printing Office, 1880.

———. "1880 U.S. Federal Population Census Napa County Original Census Forms." https://www.archives.com/imageviewer?dbId=6742&mediaId=4239981-00569&recordId=15775162:6742:886&recordType=Census.

———. "1870 Federal Census—Napa County, CA." http://us-census.org/pub/usgenweb/census/ca/napa/1870.

———. "Fourteenth Census of the United States Taken in the Year 1920, Volume III, Population 1920." Washington, D.C.: U.S. Government Printing Office, n.d.

———. "1910 U.S. Census, Bulletin 127, Chinese and Japanese in the United States 1910." Washington, D.C.: U.S. Government Printing Office, 1910.

———. *Report on Population of the United States at the Eleventh Census, 1890.* N.p.: Norman Ross Publishing, 1994.

———. "Twelfth Census of the United States Taken in the Year 1900, Population, Part 1." Washington, D.C.: U.S. Government Printing Office, 1900.

U.S. Congress. "Report of the Joint Special Committee to Investigate Chinese Immigration: February 27, 1877." Ross, 1877.

U.S. EPA, OCSPP. "Health Effects of Exposures to Mercury." Overviews and Factsheets, September 3, 2015. https://www.epa.gov/mercury/health-effects-exposures-mercury.

Wallace, Captain W.F., and Tillie Kanaga. *1901 History of Napa County.* Oakland, CA: Enquirer Print, 1901. https://lccn.loc.gov/21011771.

Wang, Dong. *The United States and China. A History from the Eighteenth Century to the Present.* Lanham, MD: Rowman & Littlefield, 2013.

Weber, Lin. *Old Napa Valley: The History to 1900.* St. Helena, CA: Wine Ventures Publishing, 1998.

Wilson, Loren. "Napa's China Town/Shuck Chan." *Historical Marker Database* (blog), April 16, 2012. https://www.hmdb.org/m.asp?m=54550.

Wong, H.K. *Gum Sahn Yun (Gold Mountain Men).* N.p.: Fong Brothers Printing Inc., 1987.

Yu, Connie Young. *Chinatown, San Jose, USA.* 3rd ed. San Jose, CA: San Jose Historical Museum Association, 2001.

INDEX

ABOUT THE AUTHOR

John McCormick grew up in Napa and is descended from five generations of Napa Valley residents. He received his bachelor's degree in engineering from the University of California, Berkeley and his master's in history from Harvard University. After a career in technology in Silicon Valley, he and his wife now own a small business in Lafayette, California.